ql

10ᵘ

THE RORSCHACH INDEX OF REPRESSIVE STYLE

Publication Number 573
AMERICAN LECTURE SERIES ®

A Monograph in
The BANNERSTONE DIVISION *of*
AMERICAN LECTURES IN PSYCHOLOGY

Edited by
MOLLY HARROWER, Ph.D.
Professor of Research in Clinical Psychology
Department of Psychiatry
Temple University School of Medicine
Philadelphia, Pennsylvania

THE
RORSCHACH INDEX
OF
REPRESSIVE STYLE

By

MURRAY LEVINE, Ph.D.
Research Psychologist

and

GEORGE SPIVACK, Ph.D.
Research Director

*The Devereux Foundation Institute
for Research and Training
Devon, Pennsylvania*

CHARLES C THOMAS • PUBLISHER
Springfield • Illinois • U.S.A.

Published and Distributed Throughout the World by
CHARLES C THOMAS • PUBLISHER
BANNERSTONE HOUSE
301-327 East Lawrence Avenue, Springfield, Illinois, U.S.A.
NATCHEZ PLANTATION HOUSE
735 North Atlantic Boulevard, Fort Lauderdale, Florida, U.S.A.

© *1964, by* CHARLES C THOMAS • PUBLISHER
Library of Congress Catalog Card Number: 64-11660

With THOMAS BOOKS careful attention is given to all details of manufacturing and design. It is the Publisher's desire to present books that are satisfactory as to their physical qualities and artistic possibilities and appropriate for their particular use. THOMAS BOOKS will be true to those laws of quality that assure a good name and good will.

Printed in the United States of America
P-4

INTRODUCTION

Unlike Athena, who is said to have sprung from the head of Zeus, full grown in battle dress, RIRS has evolved slowly, and has gone through refinement with use. Use has resulted in some change in the scoring system, and a broadened conception of the meaning and significance of the RIRS score.

The conception of the process underlying the RIRS score is still developing as far as we are concerned. What we will describe then is not a finished product ready for battle, but rather the results of what continues to be an ongoing investigation.

We set out to develop a measure of individual differences in the proneness to repress. The rationale and the principles of scoring were derived from our own clinical experience, but our thinking about Rorschach responses relies heavily on the writings of Schafer (1954), Phillips and Smith (1953), Klopfer et al. (1954), Piotrowski (1957) and Sarason (1954). In particular, the techniques of clinical analysis demonstrated by these workers helped us to discriminate and to formalize the "stimulus qualities" of Rorschach responses to which a clinician is sensitive, and upon which his judgments and interpretations are based. The manual itself formalizes our own experience. It tries to incorporate various aspects of Rorschach responses in a single scoring system.

In one sense, RIRS quantifies the subject's responses, but in another sense, RIRS tries to externalize the clinician's thinking by centering upon matters which are relevant to the clinician in the process of interpreting Rorschach tests.

The theoretical significance of RIRS began to concern us as our feeling of happy fascination that RIRS "worked" subsided. It was always clear that RIRS did not measure accomplished acts of repression, but we did seem to be getting at properties of ideation, characteristic of the individual, which were reflected in Rorschach responses. Since individuals to varying degrees characteristically exhibit certain qualities of ideation such as flow, availability and richness, we began to think of RIRS as a *style* of ideation. As a style, in George Klein's sense, whatever is measured by RIRS should possess broad generality and should be a factor in the way in which an individual comes to terms with himself and his world. As a style, RIRS should not necessarily measure "repression," but rather it should measure a property of ideation which predisposes one toward acts of repression, given the conditions for defensiveness. If RIRS does tap an important element of ideation, then this element of ideation should have ramifications in many areas of psychological functioning. It is this thesis which has served as the guide for some of the work reported here.

This volume is essentially a test manual. Its main purpose is to present the psychological "engineering" which has gone into the development of RIRS. Any one interested in using RIRS will find extensive material on reliability (scorer, retest), the stability of the scores under various conditions, and the relationship of the scores to measures of intelligence. The appendix presents medians, ranges, and interquartile ranges for a large number of clinical groups. These are not norms, since the records were obtained from a variety of sources and under varying conditions, but they may serve as a quick means of gaining "experience" with RIRS scores so that one may recognize the usual and the unusual, at least grossly. As with any psychological test measure, validation is less well developed. This is inevitable given our present state of knowledge about human personality. We have presented as much information as we have now, and tried to indicate the usefulness of RIRS as a research measure, and in clinical practice.

In the chapter on interpretation, we have allowed ourselves to depart from the necessarily constraining limits of the data to present a fuller picture of our conception of the significance of the RIRS score. We hope this section will be read seriously, but we urge our readers to understand and to appreciate that we have gone far beyond the formal data in developing our ideas on the interpretation of the score. We cannot document each statement in the last chapter in depth, but it is the last chapter which tells what our thinking is now. We hope that others will find enough of interest in this material to test RIRS in research and in clinical practice.

ACKNOWLEDGMENTS

The authors wish to express their sincerest appreciation to the large number of individuals without whose support and co-operation the present work could not have been carried out. First, we wish to express appreciation to The Devereux Foundation and its Director, Dr. Edward L. French, for giving us the freedom to follow out our own ideas. We particularly wish to express our appreciation to Molly R. Harrower who gave us both encouragement and the benefit of her rich experience. Robert G. Ballard and Zygmunt A. Piotrowski offered very helpful thoughts, Dr. Ballard offering extensive and useful criticisms of an earlier manuscript.

Over the past three years, a number of individuals have kindly let us examine Rorschach protocols and other data. Among these individuals are Louise Bates Ames, Frances Campbell, Henry Darmstadter, Paul Fiddleman, James L. Framo, Riley W. Gardner, Leo Goldberger, Nettie H. Ledwith, Eugene E. Levitt, Nathene T. Loveland, Mary McCaulley, David C. McClelland, Horace A. Page, Irving H. Paul, Alma A. Paulsen, Thomas W. Richards, Seymour B. Sarason, Rosalea A. Schonbar, Fred Schwartz, Jerome L. Singer, Richard N. Walker, Herman A. Witkin, and Harl H. Young. We also wish to express our appreciation to Richard Fletcher, E. Donald Longenecker, and Jean Smith for allowing us to use their classes to obtain data.

As internes and assistants, Harold Brecker, Anthony Graziano, Jack Quackenbush and Doreen Rothman were most helpful at different stages of our work in obtaining and analyzing Rorschach records.

Mrs. Florence Gibson, director of the McCord Library of The Devereux Foundation, obtained all the needed literature and library materials with much appreciated dispatch.

The staff of the Records Department of The Devereux Foundation, under the direction of Morgan McKean, was indispensable in obtaining records from our own files. To Mrs. Donatella Lukas goes our appreciation for her excellent secretarial service, in particular her patience with and ability to "translate" our scribbled-over manuscripts.

M.L.
G.S.

CONTENTS

LIST OF TABLES

THE RORSCHACH INDEX OF REPRESSIVE STYLE

Chapter I

CONCEPTUAL BACKGROUND: REPRESSION

THE CONCEPT OF REPRESSION is central in Freud's conceptions of psychic functioning and in his theory of psychopathology. Repression is basic to the concept of unconscious on the one side, and to the conception of ego functioning on the other. If there was not a repressive barrier, there would be no real differentiation between conscious and unconscious. The observation of acts of repression helped in the formulation of the concept of a relatively independent portion of the personality involved in coming to terms with feelings, emotions and drives on the one side, and external reality on the other. Repression has even taken its place in text books in introductory psychology as one of the major forms of forgetting.

Early in his writings, Freud used the concepts of repression and defense interchangeably, but later he conceived of defense as the general category, and repression one of its forms. A complete and scholarly review of Freud's thinking about repression has been presented recently by Madison (1961). Freud formulated a complex theoretical structure of cathectic dynamics to account for the phenomena of repression, but his full formulation is difficult to test for little or no provision is made for operational specification of the variables involved.

Freud says that repression serves the function of preventing feelings of "unpleasure;" more specifically, ". . . the essence of repression lies in simply turning something away, and keeping it at a distance from the conscious" (Freud, 1915a, p. 147). But how does the "turning away," the "keeping it at a distance from the conscious," work? Repression works through ideas. "An instinct can never become an object of consciousness—only the idea that represents the instinct can. Even in the unconscious, moreover, an instinct cannot be represented otherwise than by

3

the idea" (Freud, 1915b, p. 177). Even affects have quality as affects only when an affect is expressed through an idea. "We have asserted that in repression a severance takes place between the affect and the idea to which it belongs, and that each then undergoes its separate vicissitudes. Descriptively, this is incontrovertible; in actuality, however, the affect does not as a rule arise till the breakthrough to a new representation [idea] in the system Cs [conscious] has been successively achieved. . . . We have arrived at the conclusion that repression is essentially a process affecting ideas on the border between the system UCS [unconscious] and PCS [preconscious]. . ." (Freud, 1915b, p. 180).

Apparently as a function of the effect on ideas, the strength of the instinctive impulse is somehow diminished once its idea has undergone repression. The mechanism through which repression occurs is purportedly a withdrawal of the cathexis of energy from the conscious or preconscious idea. While the fate of the affect and the drive energies is critical for the development of substitute formation or symptoms, repression itself operates through the cognitive system and through an influence on ideas.

Dollard and Miller (1950) have translated many of the elements of Freud's views into learning theory terms. While it is not clear that Freud would accept the identity of "verbal behavior" and his concept of ideas, Dollard and Miller view repression as an automatic avoidance of verbal behavior (communicated to self or to others) when such avoidance is reinforced by reduction in anxiety. Drives, cues and responses that have never been labeled will be unconscious. Fear or anxiety may be cued by a spoken word, or by some act, and the fear may generalize to the thought or to the contemplation of the word or act. Repression in these terms, is a cessation of thinking as an avoidance response, since given thoughts (i.e., verbal communication to the self) may stand as cues that will elicit anxiety. Avoidance of the thought as a response results in successful avoidance of anxiety. Dollard and Miller explicitly identify what is conscious with what is verbally labeled. Their work emphasizes the connection between language and the phenomenon of repression.

A similar emphasis on verbal labeling is found in Rogers' (1951) theory of personality and behavior. Roger writes: "There is an even more significant type of denial which is the phenomenon the Freudians have tried to explain by the concept of repression. In this instance, it would appear that there is the organic experience, but there is no symbolization of this experience, or only a distorted symbolization, because an adequate conscious representation of it would be entirely inconsistent with the concept of self" (p. 505).

There is a rather extensive experimental literature on repression. Most of the studies deal with selective recall and perceptual defense, and these have been reviewed critically elsewhere (Zeller, 1950; Osgood, 1953; Hilgard, 1956; Eriksen, 1957). A large number of studies have succeeded in demonstrating that unpleasant or threatening material, defined in various ways, is remembered poorly or is not perceived consciously very readily. However, most such studies have not examined the process underlying "repression," nor has very much definite information been developed around the question of individual differences in repression effects. A few studies have focused explicitly upon ideational processes in relation to repression. Weisskopf-Joelson *et al.* (1957) use a concept of "label avoidance" to explain the tendency to give or to fail to give aggressive themes to specially constructed TAT cards. Subjects with repressed hostility to "father" do not give hostile themes to relatively aggressive stimuli, but they do tend to label unaggressive pictures as depicting hostile themes, compared with less repressed subjects. These findings, smacking of the psychoanalytic concept of displacement, may be incorporated into Dollard and Miller's theory (1950) by use of the concept of generalization.

Eriksen and Kuethe (1956) present findings in support of the theory of repression as avoidant verbal behavior. Electric shocks administered to arbitrarily selected associations to stimulus words led to an avoidance of the shocked associations. One group of subjects were unaware of the relationship between the shock and the words they were given, but despite the lack of awareness, the shocked associations dropped out and were replaced with new words. Associative reaction times decreased steadily for these individuals. In contrast, in subjects who were aware of the relationship between the shock and the words, reaction times first increased, and then decreased as the shocked associations dropped out. These subjects reported conscious suppression of the shocked associations. However, the experiment shows clearly that for some individuals punishment of expressed thoughts can lead to elimination of such thoughts from consciousness on a completely automatic basis.

There is ample basis in theory, and some experimental evidence to support a focus on verbal behavior as basic to the mechanism of repression. However, language has a larger role in human functioning. The recent Russian work, as reported by Luria (1961), emphasizes the role of "inner speech" in the regulation of behavior. Approaching the problem of the control and direction of behavior from a developmental view, speech is seen at first as an initiator of action or regulator of action that is initiated. Later, by its function as feedback signal, speech can be used to initiate a change in the direction of action, or indicate the point which an action is to cease. Older children learn to use speech as a self signal, providing a model of a self regulating system. Eventually action may be delayed until some internalized sequence of "planful speech" has been completed. Thus a relative independence of behavior both from the external environment and from the internal environment (feelings, drives) is seen to be dependent upon the development of thought, described in part as sequences of internalized speech. A gross similarity of this model to the model presented by Rapaport (1951) may be noted.

A limitation on ideational processes may come about as a function of continued acts of repression. Freud emphasizes that repression is not a once and for always accomplished act, but he indicates that it must constantly be renewed at the cost of continual energy expenditure. If a repression is strong, then it will generalize broadly, and pull in many ideas which stand in associative connection with the originally repressed material.

Given a number of strong repressions, it is conceivable that a gross limitation of the ideational processes would eventually ensue. An individual may come to be able to think in only the most limited areas, and in only the most limited terms. Given a history of many acts of repression, one may expect an ideationally limited individual. Given a history of many acts of repression, the very availability of language should be poor, and language should have a limited usefulness as a mediator for such an individual. It is possible that an enduring or stylistic consistency in the use of language (i.e., poor use and development of language), comes about as a function of long standing, pervasive repressions. It is also possible that a consistent, stylistic use of language may evolve early in life through particular experiences relevant to language development or neurological "givens," and that this style predisposes the individual toward repressive maneuvers (or other defenses) when anxiety arousing situations occur. In such case, both the style and particular defensive maneuver, function so as to limit thought and language behavior.

If "repression" is viewed broadly as some limitation on ideational processes, and ideational processes are necessary in giving direction, purpose and control to behavior, then the consequence of any marked limitation on ideational processes should be quite far reaching. Freud, Dollard and Miller, and Rogers all emphasize verbalization and labeling as significant determinants of action and feelings. Without adequate labeling, actions or feelings may be dominated by aroused states pressing for expression. Needs or drives may be totally inhibited by a failure of the relevant verbal mediating processes. The individual, struggling with unlabeled, and thereby unrecognized drives and feelings will not be or feel in full control of himself.

The concept of repression is obviously a powerful one, but using only limited language as a response, one cannot readily infer a history of repression. Still, using language as a response, one might very well ask whether or not other characteristics associated with limited language will appear in a variety of situations. The theory of repression provides at least one kind of mechanism to produce an individual with limited language availability. Obviously limited language may come from other sources as well, but if one could obtain some good measure of language usage, characteristics which may depend upon language usage may be associated with the measure.

Holzman (1960) has attempted to relate the defense of repression to the stylistic feature of cognition called leveling-sharpening. Leveling-sharpening is a reliable dimension of individual differences, in which the leveler, in contrast to the sharpener, diminishes the distinctiveness between a sequence of perceptual stimuli, and between elements in memory. The leveler's memories assimilate to each other, and in the end are more vague. Holzman and Gardner (1959) have presented evidence that individuals with Rorschach protocols judged as exhibiting marked reliance on the defense of repression, also tend to be levelers. Holzman concludes that repression makes use of leveling dynamics. "Repression takes its form from the way in which memory schemata are formed and stored. A memory system in which a high degree of assimilative interaction is characteristic, in which memory elements fuse with each other and lose their distinctiveness, seems to offer an effective vehicle for the defensive removal from awareness of painful memories" (p. 341).

The leveling-sharpening dimension refers to a pervasive set of individual differences, and it may even have its analogues in individual differences in characteristics of the organization of the nervous system. If leveling-sharpening is accepted as some pervasive quality of the organization of thought, it suggests the more vague and the less distinctive the thinking, the more likely the individual is to exhibit repression, given the conditions for an act of defense. Because the thinking style is general, there is the further implication that such a quality of thought may be reflected in many actions which are dependent upon the nature of ideation. The leveling-sharpening dimension may have many response indicators, but its basic property is the tendency of elements of the memory to assimilate.

We have no immediate wish to identify the measure of language we will eventually describe with the leveling-sharpening dimension, but there is no inconsistency between Holzman's view of repression as based upon leveling dynamics, and the view expressed above that repression is importantly related to the nature of language. For want of a better assumption, we are willing to follow Dollard and Miller's view that language and thought are closely related and we are willing to make the additional working assumption that the properties of language reflect the properties of thought. If the underlying thought process shows a great deal of indistinctness, it may be expected that indistinct language will also be exhibited. How these processes may be revealed in Rorschach associations is the subject of subsequent material to be presented.

Chapter II

CONCEPTUAL BACKGROUND: RORSCHACH

RORSCHACH'S (1942) original scoring system was an ingenious attempt to bring objectivity to his own intuitive and insightful appreciation of the basic projective hypothesis. The various scores which could be assigned to superficially diverse responses were assumed to represent relatively independent and homogenous psychological tendencies, although the precise meaning attributed to the scores could vary depending upon the total context of the responses.

Over the years, there have been a number of advances in Rorschach technique. There have been attempts to develop objective scales to combine the formal scores. These scales are sometimes based upon formal empirical studies, and sometimes they represent attempts to translate clinical experience into measurable and communicable terms. Many of these scales restrict themselves to using Rorschach's original scoring features in new combinations. Munroe's (1950) checklist is one such example. The checklist provides a number of "signs" which combine into a single scale measuring "adjustment." The signs are largely combinations of location and determinant scores, and various ratios between the scores. The checklist attempts to measure "adjustment" independently of diagnosis. It may be viewed as a development analogous to Rorschach's first attempts to measure "intelligence" by pointing out the scoring features which characterize the records of "intelligent" people.

Although there was a reluctance to deal with content as such, it is inconceivable that content did not influence the interpretations of the early workers. But it was not until after the second world war that content received systematic attention. Lindner (1946) published an influential paper in which contents were treated as symbols. He suggested a number of very spe-

cific interpretations for responses which appeared in certain lo-
cations. Hertzman and Pearce (1947) developed data from cases
in therapy suggesting that the content of human movement responses had deep personal significance. Building on suggestions
made by various clinicians, Due and Wright (1945) developed
a list of content signs of male homosexuality. A few years later,
Wheeler (1949) reported a validation study of the homosexual
content scale. About the same time, Elizur (1949) developed
content scales to measure anxiety and hostility. Elizur dealt
strictly with the content. In his scales, the location or the form
quality of the responses is ignored.

DeVos' (1952) score for affective symbolism is another attempt to quantify content. DeVos' system provides an index of
"affective" symbolism determined from the content of Rorschach
responses. In principle, the index of affective expression is much
like an A% or an H%. It tells us the number of responses having
affective content. DeVos does not provide a symbolic interpretation of content.

Recent textbooks have reflected the interest in content much
more than the earlier ones. Klopfer and Kelley (1942) mention
content interpretations very sparingly and Beck (1944) hardly
treats content at all. Many of the later textbooks [Klopfer *et al.*
(1954), Phillips and Smith (1953), Sarason (1954) and Piotrowski (1957)] devote extensive space to content interpretations. Holtzman *et al.* (1961) have adapted content scores such as
anxiety and barrier into their scoring.

Beyond the content, still more is observed and measured in
the Rorschach test situation. In early texts, there were only bare
hints that one should pay attention to details of the way in
which the response was offered. Klopfer and Kelley (1942) suggest that "insecurity" may be inferred from comments such as
"it might be" or "I'm not sure." Evasiveness may be reflected in
the expression of percepts in generalized terms such as "animal"
or "person." Schachtel (1945) points out how the manner of
speech, intonation, changes in speech, remarks made about the
test and other behavior may be used to understand how the subject defines the test situation. Recent texts such as Phillips and
Smith (1953), Sarason (1954), Schafer (1954) and Piotrowski

(1957) have provided a much more microscopic view of the interpretive process than was hitherto available. These clinicians reveal their associative and deductive processes in substantial detail, and in so doing they make explicit the cues in the protocols to which they respond. More and more the newer approaches stress the manner in which responses are expressed, and more and more the focus is upon the language the subject uses in giving his responses.

Piotrowski (1937) was aware of the significance of such data at a very early date. He was among the first to develop formal classification for this type of stylistic feature. In his scale for diagnosing organic disturbances of the central nervous system, Piotrowski defined the qualitative, stylistic signs of impotence, perplexity, and automatic phrasing. These three important signs describe qualities of test behavior which cannot be judged from the more usual scores.

The analysis of verbalization receives extensive treatment in Rapaport, Gill and Schafer (1946). ". . . the subject's verbalization of his response can carry within it crucial indications as to the nature of his maladjustment . . . it is a product of the subject's thought processes and is amenable to scoring, systematization and diagnostic evaluation" (p. 324). Some fifteen major categories of deviant verbalization are treated as independent signs, and one tabulates the frequency of the different types. Each type of verbalization carries its own interpretive significance. Watkins and Stauffacher (1952) developed a single scale based on these categories of deviant verbalizations. They were able to show the measure could be scored reliably and that it had validity. Powers and Hamlin (1955) supported their findings. Such a scoring system is now incorporated into the Holtzman ink blot test (1961).

Phillips and Smith (1953) have suggested that intelligence may be estimated from the subject's spontaneous vocabulary. They have also suggested one can infer social class and obsessivecompulsive characteristics from language which is excessively precise, pedantic or esoteric. These writers present many detailed suggestions in a form which invites test. Trier (1958) has reported considerable success in having judges estimate intelligence from the "most sophisticated" words from each protocol. A rating based on the Thorndike and Lorge word frequency count of the words used in giving the responses correlated .77 with full scale Wechsler-Bellevue IQs.

Holt and Havel (1960) devised a method of scoring Rorschach protocols based upon the psychoanalytic theory of primary and secondary process cognition. Arguing that any sample of mental activity may be rated along a primary-secondary process continuum, the system deals with content variables, with modes of thought and expression, and with control and defense variables. Offered as a supplement to existing scoring procedures, it is meant to depart substantially from existing scoring procedures. The system is largely dependent upon the specific contents of the responses and it is dependent upon a detailed analysis of the verbalization constituting the response.

The trend in Rorschach scoring is clearly in the direction of objectifying and quantifying so-called qualitative aspects of the record, despite the reluctance of some authorities (Beck *et al.,* 1961) to accept this trend as in the Rorschach tradition. The various scoring techniques provide explicit rules and concrete examples of the types of behavior and the types of content the clinician uses in interpreting and evaluating a record. These attempts to specify the important cues, and to quantify the critical variables help to place clinical testing on a much more scientific basis by making the techniques of analysis public and communicable.

A testing situation is useful only if it elicits a representative and pertinent sample of behavior. The more pertinent and the more representative the sample, the more accurate the predictions will be to appropriate criteria. Some years ago Thurstone (1944) included several Rorschach "perceptual" scores in his massive factor analysis of perceptual measures. Turning up a factor composed only of Rorschach scores, he suggested there may be such a thing as Rorschach specific behavior. If true, the significance of Rorschach interpretation would be severely limited.

Language and modes of expression are functions which may be observed directly in many situations. We infer thought processes from language and the modes of expression. Since we are concerned about thought processes in a variety of situations, evaluating the thought processes through the language function should be helpful in increasing the power of our interpretations. If there is any generality to behavior, we are more likely to develop useful results by observing psychological functions which clearly transcend particular situations. The current trend in scoring recognizes this principle by dealing with the verbalizations directly. The Index of Repressive Style is in keeping with the trend in Rorschach work in that it is based directly on the language of the responses.

As suggested earlier, the theory of repression and the role that labeling plays in the control of behavior provides the basis for the conception of a repressive style in the characteristics of language. The general conception holds that repressive style is a consistent characteristic of an individual and it is manifested in vague, unelaborated language which is lacking in integration and flow. The scoring manual attempts to give operational specification to this general conception as far as Rorschach responses are concerned.

We started with Rorschach responses because experience with the Rorschach test in clinical testing and in research led to an idea. As we developed a detailed scoring system, it became clear that the single response provided a good sampling unit, and the total record a reasonably extensive sample of the verbal behavior of the subject. Rorschach responses had one advantage in that the procedure provided a relatively delimited scoring unit. Samples of verbal behavior elicited by other means do not have the same natural unit of response. In narrative material, it is difficult to decide whether the word, phrase, clause, sentence, group of sentences, paragraph or entire communication is the appropriate unit of analysis.

Convenience of scoring is not the only advantage. A response to inkblots is the end product of a highly complex process in which the subject must relate the relatively uncertain figure presented by the inkblot to the much more familiar figures stored in his memory. Even those who work with inkblots extensively do not have a conception of inkblots as a class of objects in which the members are discriminated from each other and labeled. No one has this kind of articulated frame of reference for inkblots, so inkblots are related to memories of the more usual objects of our experiential and conceptual world. The instructions, "tell me what it looks like or what it reminds you of," emphasize that the subject is to relate the uncertain form of the inkblot to his memories of the more usual objects of his world.

The verbally communicated response is the end product of a process which involves perception, associative flow of ideas, images, memories, and verbal communication. However, one may infer something of the response process from the features of the verbal communication. To the extent that the language is specific, elaborated, integrated and flowing (as defined by the manual below), to that extent is the response a function of an exacting categorization of the uncertain form of the stimulus with the more certain objects represented by memory traces. The response "animal" requires that relatively few criteria be present for the stimulus to be categorized as an animal when compared to the response "Rin-Tin-Tin." For the stimulus to be categorized as Rin-Tin-Tin, it must not only have the basic animal form, but it must also imply specific form, specific size, specific color, etc. The more specific, concrete, unique term may be produced as a Rorschach response when the process of categorization involves multiple, intersecting criteria.

Concreteness and specificity of the response require a great deal of differentiation, but other elaborations of the response add to the differentiating criteria. A tree may be found anywhere, and huge stretching oaks, delicate young dogwoods, and compact evergreens may all be called trees. However the "gnarled oak with the broken branch, which used to be on my grandfather's farm" is a response in which the stimulus provided by the inkblot has been assigned to a category which requires that many highly specific criteria appear together. These criteria may be inferred from the language of the response itself. The same reasoning can be extended to the inclusion of verbs in a response. An object described in action is fixed by more than its own form. It is the object engaged in a very definite act, the act itself differentiating the object from all other members of its class not in action. The object in motion is defined as a member of a more definite sub-class.

The various scoring elements are described in the manual in terms of their relation to the overall conception of repressive style. Our general conception implies that the combination of terms reflects the process of differentiating one object or situation from another with greater or lesser precision. While we follow the general view that language provides a set of mediating responses, we are concerned with only one property of language. While others have focused on such variables as the type token ratio, or the adject-verb quotient, or details of grammatical structure, and attempted to relate these to personality variables, our scoring technique treats the elements of language as all serving a single function, that of establishing precise, delimited, multidefined conceptions of aspects of both the inner and outer worlds. Through his language, an individual imposes his own frame of reference upon his experiences, and if the language function is highly developed in the manner suggested here, then his percepts and concepts will not only be personalized, but they will also be delimited and precise in the sense they will be defined by the multiple criteria we have indicated. To the extent this is achieved, to that extent we feel that the language (and thought) is unrepressed. Responses to inkblots permit the characteristics of language and thought to be revealed in a situation in which the physical stimulus and the test instructions provide only very modest direction for categorization of the stimulus. It is for this reason that Rorschach responses may have a peculiar usefulness in helping us to understand how an individual comes to terms with himself and his world.

Chapter III

THE RORSCHACH INDEX OF
REPRESSIVE STYLE

THE RORSCHACH TEST elicits a flow of verbal associations in response to the instruction: "Tell me what you see, whatever it looks like to you." In some sense, these instructions are analogous to the "fundamental rule" of psychoanalysis that the analysand tell everything which comes to mind. When an individual agrees to take a Rorschach test, it is assumed that he also agrees to communicate his responses as fully as he can. It seems reasonable to expect that the variations in quality and content of thought which characterize repressive functioning should be directly manifested in the verbal associations to inkblots.

The first task was to define those qualities of verbalization in the "free" association part of the test that would indicate repressive functioning. In this task, we drew from the work of others in Rorschach testing, and we also used those signs of repressive functioning observable in psychotherapy as suggestions of how repressive functioning might be manifest in Rorschach free associations. We arrived at a general conception: *The more the verbalization of a Rorschach response reflects vague, impersonal and unelaborated thinking, and lacks integration and flow of ideas, the more repressive functioning has been manifest. The more the verbalization of the response is stated in specific, affectively toned terms and is characterized by a continued and developing flow of words, the less repressive functioning is indicated.*

This general conception was concretized in seven * scoring principles.

1. Specificity
2. Elaboration

---

* Originally minus responses were also scored. As a matter of convenience we have since stopped scoring these. We found the added information was not sufficient to justify the amount of time spent in checking the form quality in tables, particularly when scoring RIRS in large numbers of records for research purposes. Clinically the evaluation of minus responses is helpful in deciding whether a high score reflects decompensation of defense or creative and adaptive responses.

3. Impulse responses
4. Primary process thinking
5. Self references
6. Movement
7. Organization

Employing these principles, a scoring manual was devised. The RIRS for any Rorschach record is the mean of the distribution of scores earned by the responses given in the free association portion of the record. *Only verbalizations made during the free association period are scored,* although information from inquiry should be employed when it helps to clarify issues of scoring the response proper.* Verbalization recorded during inquiry does not enter into the scoring otherwise. All responses which are conventionally scored, are scored in this system. Each free association is scored to indicate the *absence* of repressive functioning. Thus, the *lower* the RIRS score, the *more* repressive functioning is said to characterize the individual.

SCORING PRINCIPLES

Specificity

Specificity refers to the quality of the nouns in a response. The greater the specificity, the less repressive functioning. By specificity is meant the extent to which the content refers to a unique entity, in contrast to a broadly general or vague concept. In the Rorschach situation, the response "animal" is relatively non-specific, requiring fewer criteria than the response "bear" and many fewer criteria than "Rin-Tin-Tin." By the same rule, the response "a person" is less specific than "a man," while "Fu Manchu" refers to a unique man.

By specific, is meant *idea* specific. A response like "sky" is *form* vague, but it is *idea* specific since it refers to a definite entity. This type of form vague response is scorable since the term specificity as used here does not mean form articulated as in developmental scoring of the Rorschach (Hemmendinger, 1960).

---

* There are some instances in which the inquiry produces very rich material, but the free association is sparse. We suspect that such instances may reflect response suppression, and the obtained RIRS may not be representative of Ss style of responding.

The relationship between specificity and repressive functioning is partly distilled from our clinical experience. In working with Rorschach material, we have noted that the content of the response seems to convey more to us about the person who gives it when the response is something specific. We have the feeling, rightly or wrongly, that we can sink our "clinical teeth" into such a response better if it is a more specific something. A more specific response seems to provide a perceptual and conceptual stimulus for the clinician which leads him to feel the other person has revealed something of himself. We are apt to say that the response is more personalized. In making such a statement, we are saying that drives, affective states, feelings about self or others are expressed in the response. Using a clinical orientation, if personalized material can be "read" from the response, we assume that the subject's repressive barrier has sufficiently lifted so that personalized material is guiding the response process. The less we can "read" from the response, the more we assume defensive processes have not been lifted to permit expression of personalized material.

It is also our assumption that when the response is more specific, it reflects a greater availability to consciousness of distinct and verbalizable memories and images. From a theoretical viewpoint the greater the availability of such distinct memories and images, the less the generalized tendency to repress. In discussing "repression-resistance" in therapy, Madison (1961, p. 54) describes vagueness in relating information as indicative of repressive (resistive) functioning. The patient loses the connectedness of elements and there are large gaps that remain unfilled. Holzman (1960) also speaks of the leveler, who is prone to repress, as having an undifferentiated quality in memory "schemata."

Scores for content specificity range from 0 to 2. Generally speaking, ideationally vague responses are scored zero while more specific content earns a higher score. In a few instances the scoring arbitrarily departs from the rule and this reflects our clinical judgment about the response. Content directly related to impulse areas is automatically scored 2 whether the content is specific or vague (see below).

1. *Human Percepts*

a) *Person, human form, body,* and the body parts *head, face,* and *profile* are scored *0. Torso, arm, hand, fingers, legs, back, chest,* etc. would be scored *1.*

b) Identification by sex, age, occupation, including recreational activity (e.g. *bowler,* or *runner*) is scored *1.* Each such independent identification is scored, and the scores are additive. Although age is implied in a response such as *boy, girl, man,* or *woman,* the response scores only *1.* The responses *baby, child, infant,* etc. are scored *2.* A specifically named person such as *George Washington, Santa Claus, Teddy Roosevelt,* etc. is scored 2.

c) Human-like or mythological forms such as *monster, dwarf, witch, cherub, giant, angel,* and the like are scored *2.* The response *creature* is scored *0. Silhouette* and *shadow* score *1. Puppet* or *cartoon* character is scored *1.* A specifically named puppet or cartoon character, such as *Pinocchio,* would be scored 2.

d) If one part of a possessive form is scorable, then the whole response may be scored one point.

Ex. Card II, Person's head.

Sc. *Person's* (0), *head* (0). Total score = 0.

Ex. Card II, Lady's head.

Sc. *Lady's* (1), *head* (0). Total score = 1.

If both the possessive and the object are scorable, the response is scored accordingly.

Ex. Card I, Woman's finger.

Sc. *Woman's* (1), *finger* (1). Total score = 2.

The possessive form his or her's is not scored, but the possessive *my* may be scored *1* as a Self Reference (see below).

2. *Animal Percepts*

a) *Animal, animal skin, skin, pelt, insect, bird, fish, dog,* are scored *0.*

b) Specific creatures such as *bear, bear skin, cat, collie, scotty, poodle, sheep, lion, rodent, bug, beetle, cricket, canary, eagle, shark, alligator, flounder, bat, butterfly, fly, dragon fly* etc. all score *1.*

c) Possessive forms follow the same rules as outlined above under Human Percepts (1.d).

d) Indication of the young of the species scores 2. Examples are *puppy, lamb, pollywog, cub, chick,* etc.

e) Cartoon animals such as *Donald Duck,* or *Sylvester Cat* or puppet animals are scored 2.

3. *Anatomy*

a) *Bones, internal organ, your insides* and similar vague anatomy are scored 0.

b) Specific bones (e.g., *ribs, vertebrae, pelvis,* etc.) and specific anatomical detail (e.g., *lungs, kidney, spinal column,* etc.) are scored 1. *Skeleton* is scored 1.

c) *X-ray* given alone is scored 1. An *X-ray* of something is treated as an elaboration scoring 1.

4. *Art and Design*

a) A *painting, a drawing, a design, art work,* and similar vague and unspecified art references are scored 0. *Inkblot, paint,* and responses which are color naming or card description score 0.

b) Specific subtypes such as *water color, impressionist painting, modern art,* or *oil painting,* etc. are scored 1.

c) Art products which are identified with the name of the artist are scored 2.

Ex. Card X. Reminds me of a painting by Dali.

Sc. *Painting* (0), *Dali* (2). Total score = 2.

5. *Botany*

a) *Tree, plant, bushes, flower,* or *leaf* are scored 0.

b) Specific trees (e.g., *pine tree, Christmas tree*), specific flowers (e.g., *orchid, daffodil, sweet pea*), leaves (e.g., *maple leaf*) and *grass* and *weeds* are scored 1.

c) Parts of a flower (e.g., *petals, stem, pistil, stamen* etc.) and parts of trees (e.g., *limb, trunk, roots, bark,* etc.) are scored 1. *Seed* or *bud* also score 1.

6. *Clothing*

a) The response *clothing* is scored 0.

b) Usual articles of clothing (e.g., *shoes, boots, bow tie, ribbon, jacket,* etc.) are scored 1.

c) *Brassiere, corset, panties, slip,* or any specific under-garment of either sex is scored 2, under impulse response, sex (see below).

d) The term *dressed* in a phrase such as *"dressed in a jacket"* is not scored. The term *"dressed up"* to imply "fancy" would score *1* as an elaboration.

7. *Clouds*

a) *Cloud* is scored *0.*

b) A specific cloud such as *cumulus* or *thunderhead* is scored *1.*

c) The response *sky* scores *1.*

8. *Fire*

a) *Fire, flames,* or *smoke* are scored *1.*

9. *Household and Objects*

a) *Furniture, tools, decoration, things,* etc. score *0.*

b) *Lamp, chair, curtain, stove, bench, pliers,* etc. score *1.*

c) Objects (true also for other content categories) which are ordinarily referred to by two words will score *1* usually (e.g., *bow tie, lawn mower*).

10. *Landscape, Geography, and Mineral*

a) *Map, aerial photograph, rocks, water, mountain, scenery,* and other such vague references are scored *0.*

b) Geographical details (e.g., *island, coast, bay, lake, sea, ocean,* etc.) are scored *1.*

c) A specific place (e.g., *Pike's Peak, Old Faithful, Grand Canyon,* etc.) is scored *2.*

d) *Coral,* or *coral reef,* and specific stones such as *quartz,* or specific minerals such as *iron* or *oil* are scored *1.*

e) *Rocky, watery, mountainous,* etc. used as adjectives are scored *1* under elaboration.

11. *Complex Responses*

If the main response content scores *0* but integral parts of the main responses are specified, *and these parts are scorable,* the response is scored *1*, no matter how many scorable parts are mentioned. If some part has direct impulse significance, the part is scored additionally.

> Ex. A person, there's his *head*, his *arms* and *feet*. Scored *1*.
> A flower, you can see the *petals* and the *stem*. Scored *1*.
> A person, there's the head, face and body. Scored *0*.
> A person, there's his head and *eyes*. You can see the *buttocks*. Scored *3* (eyes 1 and buttocks 2).

12. *Miscellaneous*

In general, most responses referring to natural and man made objects (with the exception of responses similar to *"instrument"* or *"thing"*) which are not treated elsewhere in the manual, are scored *1*. Comparison of questionable responses with scoring examples should clear up the questions. When in doubt, it is suggested that the response be scored conservatively.

Elaboration

1. The greater the elaboration of the response in terms of adjectives and adverbs and phrases serving such grammatical functions, the greater the degree of personalized expression incorporated in the response, and the less the repression. Again, the relationship between *elaboration* and *repressive functioning* is partly distilled from our introspections about the process of making clinical interpretations of the Rorschach test. In most instances such elaborations seem to be the elements which give the affective toning to the response, and in other ways increase the degree of personalization of response. For example, the response "bird" to Card V is less personalized than a "big, powerful bird," and we can assume less about the affective state of the person who gives the response "tree" to Card IV than the person who calls Card IV "a dying tree with drooping branches."

In most instances it is the adjectives which provide the affective component of the response, and in keeping with Cliff's (1959) demonstration that adverbs multiply the scale value of adjectives, adverbs are also scored. We assume that when such elaborations are made, not only has there been an affective reaction on the part of the individual, but the verbal derivative of the affect has come into consciousness. The presence of these affective derivatives indicates that repressive functioning is low, since one defensive function of repression is to prevent the entry into consciousness of such verbal images.

2. Adjectives and adverbs, and phrases which are essentially adjectival or adverbial in function, are *each* scored *1*, and the points are added into the total for the response. These words and phrases often reflect aspects such as size, emotional state, physical state, beauty, ugliness, weakness, physical strength, etc. Color naming is specifically excluded, although in a response such as "a black butterfly," the black may be scored.

Ex. Card IV. A huge, towering man.

Sc. *Huge* (1), *towering* (1), *man* (1). Total score = 3.

3. Elaborations which reflect card properties directly are not scored. Phrases such as "the upper part" or "in the green there is" are not scorable.

4. Certain adjectives implying *deterioration* are scored 2. These will usually refer to anatomy responses, but are scored 2 wherever they appear. Examples of adjectives scoring 2 are: *decayed, ripped, torn, broken, mutilated, sick, dead, deformed,* etc.

5. Adjectives referring directly to impulse areas (see below) are scored 2, but are entered in the appropriate impulse column of the scoring sheet rather than under elaboration.

Ex. Card II. A bloody paw.

Sc. *Bloody* (2, under impulse, hostile), *paw* (1). Total score = 3.

6. *Medical book,* is scored 1, even if the content itself is not scorable (e.g., a diagram (0) such as you would see in a medical book (1).) An *x-ray* of something is also treated as an adjective and scored 1 under elaboration.

7. Sometimes a number of essentially synonymous terms are given in qualifying any response. Where this occurs, the synonymous terms are considered to express the quantity of affect involved. Each synonymous term is to be treated then as if it were an adverb and scored 1 additional point accordingly.

Ex. Card IX. A man. He's mad, angry, enraged.

Sc. *Man* (1), *mad* (2, under impulse, hostile), *angry* (1, under elaboration), *enraged* (1, under elaboration). Total score

= 5. Note that this response scores in exactly the same fashion as if the response was "A *man*. He's *very, very angry*."

Ex. Card II. Head of a baby lamb.

Sc. *Head* (0), *baby* (2, under elaboration), *lamb* (1, under elaboration). Total score = 3.

8. If a detail which is an integral part of a scorable main response is specified, the detail itself is scored 0 for specification. If some other scorable *elaboration* of the detail is given, then this elaboration is scored.

Ex. Card IV—A man, you see his head, feet, arms.

Sc. *man* (1), Total—*1*.

Ex. Card IV—A man, he has big feet and withered arms.

Sc. *man* (1), *big* (1) and *withered* (2, under deterioration, see 4 above), Total—*4*.

9. See Movement responses, below, for treatment of past tenses.

Impulse Responses

Any direct reference to sexuality, hostility, anality, or dependency in a response reflects lessened repressive functioning. It is assumed that repressions are maintained to keep just such impulse derivatives from consciousness. The presence of such ideation in the Rorschach thus implies a lessening of repressive functioning. This lessening of repression may take place when the individual accepts and incorporates the idea, when there is a defensive failure, or when there is isolation of the thought from its affect.

Because repressive defenses are generally directed against such direct impulse representation, the appearance of impulse material "in the raw" is weighted in the scoring system. The score of 2 for impulse response is entered in the appropriate impulse column of the scoring sheet.

1. *Sex*

a) Any sex content as *penis* or *vagina* is scored 2.

b) Sex or other impulse content in a *verb* is scored 3, two under the appropriate impulse column, and *1* in the movement column.

Ex. Card X. Two men masturbating.

Sc. *Men* (1), *Masturbating* (3, enter 2 under sex, impulse, and 1 under movement). Total score = 4.

c) The content of the response must be given clearly to be scored. The sexual term must be used directly.

Ex. Card VII. A woman's parts.

Sc. *Woman* (1, under elaboration), *parts* (0). Total score = 1.

2. *Dependency*

a) Direct oral references including *food, mouth, beak, eating utensils, breast, mother, stomach, fetus, cannibal,* etc. are all scored 2.

b) Dependency content in a *verb* (e.g., *sucking, eating*) is scored 3 (i.e., 2 for impulse, 1 for movement) as with other impulse content.

3. *Anal*

a) All direct anal references including *anus, rectum, buttocks, feces, rear end,* and responses such as *mud,* or *dirt,* are all scored 2. *Smear* or *smudge* as an unelaborated response scores 0.

4. *Hostility*

a) *Attack, biting, tearing, arguing, fighting, blood, angry looks, mutilation, weapons, war scenes, war instruments* including *shield, fort, gun, holster* etc. are scored 2.

b) *Bomb, A-Bomb, H-Bomb,* and *explosion* all score 2. Explosion is an exception to the rule that impulse material in verb form scores a total of 3. *Explosion* alone scores 2; *H-Bomb explosion* or *exploding* would score 3, 2 under hostility and 1 under movement.

Responses Reflecting Primary Process Thinking

1. *Primary process thinking* is noted in such qualities of thought as condensations, displacements, physiognomic impressions, and magical notions and is guided mainly by affects and drives. The presence of such thinking in the Rorschach responses thus reflects a lower degree of repression. These responses are confabulations (DW), contaminations, position responses, symbolic and abstract responses. These responses appear rather in-

frequently, and for their definitions reference can be made to Beck (1944). Such responses are scored 2 points.

2. *The Abstract Response*

a) The abstract response (Beck's *Ab* content category) is scored 2. These responses often express moods or emotions, or they tend to be associations to blot characteristics rather than percepts as such.

Ex. Card IV. It reminds me of death, the blackness.

Sc. *Death* (2). Total score = 2.

b) If scorable elaborations are present in an abstract response, then these elaborations are scored and added to the total for the response.

Ex. Card X. Springtime, it's gay.

Sc. *Springtime* (2, under symbolic), *gay* (1, under elaboration). Total score = 3.

Self References

Such statements reflect the existence of personalized feelings and memories in consciousness, and indicate a lower degree of repression. These statements usually take the form of direct expression of affect (e.g., "I feel nervous taking this test"), or the recollection of something that relates associatively to the response given. These remarks and comments are usually recorded verbatim, although not treated as responses in conventional Rorschach scoring systems. Some of these remarks are scored in the present system; the score for the remark is usually added to the total for the response *just prior* to the remark. If the remark is made before the first response to a card has been given, the score for the remark is added to the total for the *next* response.

1. Any statement that refers directly to the subject's own feeling state during testing is scorable. Expressions of *fear, nervousness, uneasiness, joy, wishes* or *desire, pleasure, anger, tiredness, boredom, frustration* or *conflict* are included and score 1 for each such separate statement. The reference to the subject's feeling state should be a direct one, and not inferred from his remarks or his behavior. Usually, the complete sentence will be the unit to be scored. These responses communicate something about the current psychological state of the testee.

Ex. "I'm tired. I hope we finish soon."

Sc. *Tired* (1), *hope* (1). Total score = 2.

2. A remark which indicates a personal memory associated with the response, is scored *1*. In general, these remarks reflect a flow of associations. Since statements involving recall of previous examinations are specific to those who are retested, such remarks are *not* scorable.

Ex. Card V. A bat. Once a bat flew into my room when I was a child.

Sc. *Bat* (1), *entire memory* (1). Total score = 2.

3. A remark which is an "interpretation" of the response scores *1*. Again, in this type of remark, associations are flowing freely.

Ex. Card III. A shadow of a man. That's like me, I've just been a shadow of myself since I've been sick.

Sc. *Shadow* (1), *man* (1), *entire interpretation* (1). Total score = 3.

4. Statements which are self-critical, critical of the test, of the examiner, or of particular responses are scored zero (e.g., "I'm stupid," "This is a lousy test," "You're no help to me at all," "It's not a very good bird," "My imagination is not very good)." These responses generally block the associative flow.

5. A zero score is given for simple statements of inability, for statements in which the locus of the problem is placed in the test, or for sign-off formulas (e.g., "I can't think of anything else," "I can't see any more," "Nothing comes to my mind," "I'm afraid that's all," "This card is the hardest one yet)." Again the flow of responses is stopped by such remarks.

6. Requests for structuring or for further instructions are scored zero (e.g., "Is it all right to turn the card?" "Do you want more than one response?" "Should I tell you the first thing that comes to my mind?").

Movement Responses

The more M the less repressive functioning is said to be in operation, since M reflects personal fantasy, or trial action, and may be considered a direct verbal derivative of affects and drives. FM and m are assumed to be the same as M for purposes of scoring RIRS.

1. Movement responses are scored one point each, whether or not the response scores on any other basis. The fact that a response would score *M* by usual Rorschach standards is not sufficient to score it here as movement. To be scorable *the verb must be stated in the free association portion of the test.* Scores for movement are added to the scores assigned to a response for other reasons.

2. If a *verb* scores under the impulse section it also scores as movement.

Ex. Card II. Two men fighting.

Sc. *Men* (1), *fighting* (3) (2 under impulse, hostile; 1 under movement.) Total score = 4.

3. No score for movement is given for phrases such as "facing," "coming out of," "attached to," etc., when these phrases just imply position.

4. Sometimes S will give more than one verb in a response. In the usual Rorschach scoring, only one *M* is counted. However, if the movement verbs are different, and not merely synonymous, and if the one verb does not necessarily imply the presence of the second (so that the second verb is superfluous) then each verb is scored and the scores are additive.

Ex. Card I. Two witches holding a girl who is struggling.

Sc. *Witches* (2), *holding* (1), *girl* (1), *struggling* (1). Total score = 5.

Ex. Card III. Two men bowling. They are holding balls.

Sc. *Men* (1), *bowling* (1), *holding* (not scored), *balls* (1). Total score = 3.

5. A phrase such as "trying to run" or "trying to climb" is treated as a single movement response.

6. Past tenses are scored as elaborations rather than as movement responses.

Ex. Card II. It looks as if his leg *was chopped off.*

Sc. *Leg* (1, under specificity), was *chopped off* (2, under impulse, hostility). Total score = 3.

Ex. Card III. Two men, they look as if they had been running.

Sc. *Men* (1), *had been running* (1, under elaboration). Total score = 2.

Associational Flow

The more ease with which associational connections are made, and ideas remain in consciousness to shape and *organize* responses, the less repressive functioning is operative. The scoring for associational flow is somewhat more difficult than the scoring for other elements. Usually associational flow is observed in the more complex Rorschach responses. Five instances of "associational flow" are given below. Associational flow is not scored as a separate category since the elements making for flow (or its absence) can be handled within the categories already described (e.g., specificity, elaboration, etc.). When associations flow readily, the score for any specific response is increased as indicated.

1. If a detail is included in a response, the detail being *separate and distinct* from the main response content, and the subject states a definite relationship between the detail and the main response or such a relationship is implied, the detail is scored and added to total response score. In the usual Rorschach scoring, such a detail may be scored as a separate response, but not so under the present system.

Ex. Card III. A woman. She has a basket.

Sc. *Woman* (1), *basket* (1), Total = 2.

Ex. Card III. Two men bending over—there's a butterfly in between them.

Sc. *Men* (1), *bending over* (1), Total = 2.
Butterfly (1), Total = *1.*

(This response is scored as two separate responses since there is no stated or implied relationship between *men* and *butterfly*).

2. Responses usually considered precision alternatives, and responses which show a "shaping" or a "working through" quality, or which involve a defensive denial with substitution of a different percept, are scored as specific additions and elaborations of the initial response rather than as separate responses. Mere repetition of a response or elaborations are not scored. Precision alternatives are defined as Beck (1944) defines these.

Ex. Card V. "A vampire bat. No, it looks more like a butterfly or a moth."

Sc. *Vampire* (1), *bat* (1), *butterfly* (1), *moth* (1)—Total = *4.*

3. Additions to a response occurring further on in the record, *when scorable*, are added to the total for the response *immediately preceding the scorable addition*. The additional element is assumed to be determined more by where it comes in the sequence of responses than by association to the initial response to which it belongs. While it makes little difference in the final RIRS score itself where the addition is scored, conceivably such points could affect any analysis based on sequence of scores.

4. When a vague W response is given, but is spontaneously elaborated or its elements are described as meaningfully related or interacting, the entirety is scored as one response.

The vague W is scored for whatever it contains and then the spontaneously given specifications and elaborations are scored as necessary.

Ex. Card X. An under water scene. There are fish swimming and here's an octopus with long tentacles grabbing a greenish fish trying to escape it, and some sea weed attached to this coral.

Sc. *Underwater* (1), *scene* (0), *fish* (0), *swimming* (1), *octopus* (1), *long* (1), *tentacles* (not scored), *grabbing* (1), *greenish* (1), *fish* (0), *trying to escape* (1), *sea weed* (1), *coral* (1). Total = 9.

Ex. Card X. A lot of bugs. Here's a bug and here's an ant. Up here are two insects fighting. It all looks like a lot of bugs.

Sc. bugs (1). Total = *1*.

ant (1). Total = *1*.

insects (0), fighting (3). Total = *3*.

This is scored as three separate responses, since the elements comprising the vague W have no meaningful or active connectedness. Rather, they are discreet and unrelated.

5. Responses which are clearly perseverations and which are repeated more than three times in a record are not scored after the third repetition, unless some new scorable element enters. The perseverated response is then given a score of *0* with the total for any *new* scorable elaborations added to the zero.

6. Rejection of a card (seen as a complete block in associational flow) is counted as a response with a score of *0*. If a scorable verbatim remark is made in relation to a card rejection, the verbatim remark is "added" to the zero score for that card.

Ex. Card IX. I don't see anything there. Boy I feel nervous. I hope this is the last card.

Sc. *I feel nervous* (1), *I hope* (1). Total = 2.

CALCULATING THE RORSCHACH INDEX
OF REPRESSIVE STYLE

RIRS is the mean of all scorable responses following the system outlined above. In calculating it, one merely gets the total
of all the scores in the record and divides by the total number of
responses. It will be noted that *RIRS* thus controls for *R*, and
that a standard deviation of the distribution of response scores
can be calculated for each individual record. Since the scores in
the present system indicate a lack or lowering of repression, the
higher the *RIRS*, the lower the repressive barrier being measured.
The interpretive value of the standard deviation of *RIRS* must
await other research with *RIRS*. However, the ability of the
present scoring system to generate both a mean and a distribution implies that statistical tests can be made in comparing the
scores for a single individual for tests taken at different times.

An Illustrative Case

A Rorschach protocol is scored below in order to demonstrate
the use of the scoring system outlined in this manual, and the
use of the Scoring Sheet devised by the authors. The Scoring
Sheet in the main is self-explanatory. The columns headed "specificity" and "elaboration," might be confused occasionally. The
score for the main content of the response plus any other *nouns*
scorable under the conventions outlined are entered under "specificity." The total score for all adjectives as elaborations of the
main content or added content are entered under "elaboration."
In the following case, not only will the scores for each element
in a response be given, but the appropriate column on the Scoring Sheet will be specified. Following the completed record, the
completed Scoring Sheet is given, with the calculated *RIRS* and
its *SD*.

The case is of a 16-year-old girl of above average intelligence,
diagnosed Personality Disorder. Only the free association is given,
since this is all that is needed for scoring *RIRS* in this case.

Card I.   "A witch with wings, dancing with a lady . . . **taking
her by the arms.**"

Response 1:
witch — 2 for *specificity*
wings — 1 for *specificity* since wings are not a usual part of a witch and thus they are not mere enumeration of parts of *witch*.
dancing — 1 for *movement*
lady — 1 for *specificity*
taking her — 1 for *movement*
by the arms — 0 for *specificity* as an addition of an integral part to *lady*
Total Response Score — 6.

Card II.   "Turkeys dancing."
Response 2:
Turkeys — 1 for *specificity*
dancing — 1 for *movement*
Total Response Score — 2.

Card III.   "Two cannibals trying to boil somebody in a pot. Flames are falling out from under the pot. They look like circus acrobats."
Response 3:
Two cannibals — 2 for *impulse, oral*
trying to boil — 3, 1 for *movement*, and 2 for *impulse, hostile*
somebody — 0 for *specificity*
in a *pot* — 2, as an additional *impulse, oral*
Flames — 1 for specificity
falling out — 1 for *movement*
from under the pot — not scored, since it is simple repetition of a previously scored element.
circus acrobats — 2, 1 for *specificity* (acrobats), and 1 for *elaboration* (circus); this is scored and added to the total since it involves a kind of "shaping" of the main content.
Total Response Score — 11.

Card IV.   "Looks like a giant with a club."
Response 4:
giant — 2 for *specificity*, because of the *human-like* form

club — 2 as an *impulse, hostile*
Total Response Score — 4.

Card V.   "Looks like a magnified butterfly. Extra long wings."
Response 5:
Butterfly — 1 for *specificity*
magnified — 1 for *elaboration* of *butterfly*
extra — 1 for *elaboration* of *long*
long — 1 for *elaboration* of *wings*
wings — is not scorable, since it is only an enumeration of an integral part of *butterfly*
Total Response Score — 4.

Card VI.   "Looks like the top of one of these Indian poles. Some skins — on top of the skins there are Indian feathers." (Although it appears from the free association that this may be two responses, the inquiry indicated this was a combinatory W response.)
Response 6:
top — 0 for *specificity*
pole — 1 for *specificity*
Indian — 1 for elaboration of *pole*
skins — 0 for *specificity*
feathers — 1 for *specificity*
Indian — 0 for *elaboration*, because of simple repetition
Total Response Score — 3.

Card VII.   "This looks like two old ladies with feathers in their hair. No bodies. Balancing on rocks."
Response 7:
old — 1 for *elaboration* of *ladies*
ladies — 1 for *specificity*
feathers — 1 for *specificity*
hair — 0 for *specificity*, since it is an integral part of the ladies
No bodies — 1 for *elaboration of ladies*
balancing — 1 for *movement*

rocks — 0 for *specificity*
Total Response Score — 5.

Card VIII.   "It looks like two raccoons climbing up a steep moun-
             tain."
             Response 8:
             raccoons — 1 for *specificity*
             climbing up — 1 for *movement*
             steep — 1 for *elaboration* of *mountain*
             mountain — 0 for *specificity*
             Total Response Score — 3.

Card IX.   "Looks like two witches on top . . . being pushed up
             on a rock by two monsters standing on pink clouds."
             Response 9:
             witches — 2 for *specificity*
             pushed up — 1 for *movement*
             rock — 0 for *specificity*
             monsters — 2 for *specificity*
             standing — 1 for *movement*
             pink — 1 for *elaboration* of *clouds*
             clouds — 0 for *specificity*
             Total Response Score — 7.

Card X.   "This looks like crabs. And a caterpillar. Sea horses.
             Clams having a dance."
             Response 10:
             crabs — 1 for *specificity*
             Total Response Score — 1.
             Response 11:
             caterpillar — 1 for *specificity*
             Total Response Score — 1.
             Response 12:
             Sea horses — 1 for *specificity*
             Total Response Score — 1.
             Response 13:
             clams — 1 for *specificity*
             having a dance — 1 for *movement*
             Total Response Score — 2.

Name:_____   Date:_____

Sex: Female   Birth Date: Age 16

Rorschach Index of Repressive Style Scoring Sheet *
Murray Levine and George Spivack
Devereux Foundation Institute for Research & Training

Card #	R	Movement	Specificity	Elaboration	Impulse Resp. hostile	oral	anal	sexual	Symbolic	Confab.	Contam.	Position	Self Ref.	Total Resp. Score	Total Card Score	Total Resp. Sc. Squared
I	1	2	4											6	6	36
II	2	1	1											2	2	4
III	3	2	2	1	2	4								11	11	121
IV	4		2		2									4	4	16
V	5		1	3										4	4	16
VI	6		2	1										3	3	9
VII	7	1	2	2										5	5	25
VIII	8	1	1	1										3	3	9
IX	9	2	4	1										7	7	49
X	10		1											1		1
	11		1											1		1
	12		1											1		1
	13	1	1											2	5	4
	14															
	15															
	16															
	17															
Sum														50	292	

$$\frac{RIRS}{} = \frac{\text{Sum total resp. score}}{\text{Total R}} = \frac{50}{13} = 3.85 \qquad \sigma = \sqrt{\frac{N\,\Sigma\,X^2 - (\Sigma\,X)^2}{N}}$$

$= \sqrt{\dfrac{13(292) - (50)^2}{13}} = 2.77$

Chapter IV

RELIABILITY AND STABILITY

Rᴇʟɪᴀʙɪʟɪᴛʏ ᴏꜰ ꜱᴄᴏʀɪɴɢ is a primary consideration in evaluating any technique for quantifying projective material. Jensen (1959) writes that scorer reliability is rarely reported in the literature on the Rorschach test, it being considered secondary to the reliability of interpretation. In one study, cited by Jensen, the average phi coefficient for scorer reliability was .64. Rohrer *et al.* (1955) have reported scorer reliabilities for group Rorschachs administered to Navy and Marine personnel. Median scorer reliability for the various scoring elements and for the various techniques of scoring was about .77.

SCORER RELIABILITY

RIRS has been subjected to several tests of scorer reliability, with consistently good results. Table I summarizes these studies.

TABLE I

Sᴄᴏʀᴇʀ Rᴇʟɪᴀʙɪʟɪᴛʏ

Scorers	Number of Records	Type of Records and Subjects	Statistic	Coefficient
Co-authors	20	Individual Behn Blots (Adolescents)	r	.95
Res. Asst. and Sr. Author	10	Group Rorschachs (College Students)	rho	.98
Four Internes	7	Individual Rorschachs (Adolescents)	Kendall's W	.98
Interne and Sr. Author	14	Individual Rorschachs (Children)	rho	.96

Using the co-authors, the scoring system was tested on a set of twenty individually administered Behn Rorschachs. Despite the fact that the Behn tends to yield a rather restricted range of scores, the reliability of scoring, as represented by the product moment correlation coefficient was quite high. However, we noted that one of us consistently derived somewhat higher scores than the other. (Mean scorer A = 1.24; mean scorer B = 1.49.) This small difference proved largely the result of a different interpretation of the precision alternative responses. In a subsequent revision of the manual, precision alternative responses were defined more strictly according to Beck's (1944) criteria.

Reliability based on the work of coworkers is not an adequate estimate of the utility of a manual, since coworkers have had a great deal of opportunity to learn each other's thinking about scoring. We turned to our internes to discover how well the manual served. Four internes were asked to study the manual and then to score two or three protocols. These protocols were discussed in a group and scoring differences were ironed out. The four internes proceeded to score seven additional records independently. A concordance analysis (Siegel, 1956) showed the reliability to be .98. These data were further analyzed for differences between scorers by the rank method developed by Kramer (1956). There were no significant differences among the four internes.

The scoring system's reliability was tested further with group Rorschachs. A research assistant, who had had experience with the technique and who had been trained informally in the use of the technique by one of us, scored ten randomly selected group Rorschachs. The same records were scored independently by one of us. The rank order correlation proved to be .98, but once again there was some tendency for a small constant error to appear. The scores for one scorer were consistently higher than for the other scorer. These differences again seemed to be due to factors involved in scoring precision alternatives. In the absence of a complete inquiry, as was true in the group Rorschachs, it was often difficult to decide whether a response was truly a precision alternative or not.

A final test was made when another interne was introduced to the scoring system. This time the protocols were from six and seven year old children. Because they had been administered for experimental purposes, there was no inquiry. The interne read through the manual, and then scored six records independently.

After discussion of these six records, one of us and the interne scored fourteen additional records independently. The rank order correlation for the fourteen records was .96, while the means and ranges for the two scorers were highly similar (means = 1.66 and 1.73; ranges = .64-3.47 and .78-3.21).

Scoring reliability is obviously adequate. The system can be learned readily and applied to a wide variety of inkblot tests. We have applied the scoring technique to individual records using the Rorschach blots, and the Behn blots, to self administered records using the Harrower blots, to group administered records using the Rorschach blots, and to group administered records using the Holtzman blots. Our experience suggests that reliability of scoring is uniformly high.

Some words of caution are in order. Some scorers may have a small "constant error," assigning somewhat higher scores than others. These scoring problems most often seem to involve the precision alternatives, and in scoring these should be treated carefully. One should adopt a general rule: when in doubt, score conservatively. Score as if the responses were truly separate. Because there is the possibility of a constant error, checks for this type of error are in order when protocols are scored by different examiners. Although scorer reliability is unquestionably good, the possibility of a systematic scoring bias makes blind scoring preferable in research studies. This is particularly true when test-retest data are being considered and change in the level of the scores is the issue.

RETEST RELIABILITY

A critical characteristic of any measuring instrument is its reliability. An excellent discussion of the problems involved in determining reliability in the Rorschach test is provided by Holzberg (1961). In his review, Jensen (1959) cites split half reliabilities ranging from .33 to .97 for different scoring categories (e.g., M, CF, etc.). Average split half reliability coefficients for scores range from .52 to .84 for different forms of the test, and in different studies. Jensen reports retest reliabilities for various scoring factors, in varying populations, and with varying time intervals between testings, ranging from .13 to .97. Obviously no one figure adequately represents the retest reliability of Rorschach data.

Alternate forms of inkblot tests have been used to study retest reliability. Alternate form reliability coefficients employing the Behn inkblots for the usual Rorschach scoring categories have ranged from -.05 to .86, in different studies. Average retest coefficients for all scoring elements have ranged from .41 to .65 in the studies reported by Jensen. This material is cited in order to provide some perspective for evaluating the reliability of RIRS.

The retest reliability of RIRS has been studied extensively. Through the kindness and cooperation of other investigators, we have been able to accumulate retest data on more than 350 Ss involving some 2000 Rorschach protocols. These records were taken under a wide variety of conditions, using varying forms of the tests, involving varying time periods and covering several different populations. The results are summarized in Table II.

When *different sets of inkblots* are used, and the conditions of administration remain constant, the reliability coefficients range between .50 and .67 (Table II, lines 1, 2, 3). *Individual and group administered* Rorschachs yield about the same level of reliability (Table II, line 4). With the exception of the small group of Ss who were tested under waking and hypnotic conditions (Table II, line 6a), *radical changes in testing conditions* produce a relatively reliable response, despite the fact that the mean scores change significantly in some instances (see below). Reliability coefficients range from .38 to .91 (Median = .78), even after exposure to such stringent conditions as hypnotically induced anxiety, threat, sleep deprivation and instructions to give completely new and different responses.

When the same form of the inkblots is administered under the same conditions with a relatively short period intervening, (Table II, lines 7 and 8a) reliability coefficients range from .74 to .92, the median of four coefficients being .88.

We may safely conclude that the style of response measured by RIRS is quite stable for periods as long as three months. Despite fairly radical alterations in blots, and conditions of administration, Ss tend to maintain their relative rank order quite well

TABLE II

TEST-RETEST CORRELATIONS UNDER VARIOUS CONDITIONS

	Group	N	Form of Admin.	Time Intervening	Reliability Coefficient	p
1)	Adult, male Unitarian ministers (Harrower 1959)	22	Ror. and Harrower blots, Self admin.	Same day	.67	< .01
2)	Emotionally disturbed adolescents	20	Individ. admin. Ror. and Behn blots	Three months or less	.67	< .01
3a)	Normal college females (Schwartz & Kates, 1957)	12	Individ. admin. Ror. and Behn blots, preceding and following stress	Two weeks or less	.50	<.10 > .05
b)	Normal college females (Schwartz & Kates, 1957)	12	Individ. admin. Ror. and Behn blots, simple repetition	Two weeks or less	.50	<.10 > .05
4)	Student nurses, female (Harrower-Erickson & Steiner, 1945)	68	Individ. and group Ror. blots	One week	.60	< .01
5)	Normal male adults (Weiner, Brown & Kaplan, 1956)	10	Individ. admin. Ror. blots. Instructed to give "new and different responses" on second admin.	Two days	.78	.01
6a)	Normal adults (Levitt & Grosz, 1960)	12	Ror. blots, Hypnosis vs. waking	Same day	.38	NS
b)	Normal adults (Levitt & Grosz, 1960)	12	Ror. blots, Hypnosis vs. hypnotically induced anxiety	Same day	.51	.05
c)	Normal adults (Levitt & Grosz, 1960)	12	Ror. blots, Waking vs. hypnotically induced anxiety	Same day	.78	.01
7)	Male nurses (Harrower-Erickson & Steiner, 1945)	20	Group admin. Ror. blots	One week	.91	< .01

TABLE II (*Cont.*)

TEST-RETEST CORRELATIONS UNDER VARIOUS CONDITIONS

	Group	N	Form of Admin.	Time Intervening	Reliability Coefficient	p
8a)	Normal male adults (Loveland & Singer, 1959)	25	Ror. blots, Control *S*s	1st to 4th day 1st to 7th day 4th to 7th day	.85 .74 .92	< .01 < .01 < .01
b)	Normal male adults (Loveland & Singer, 1959)	25	Ror. blots, before and after sleep deprivation	Four days	.91	< .01
			before and after recovery from sleep deprivation	Seven days	.81	< .01
			after sleep deprivation and after recovery	Three days	.83	< .01

on reexamination. The reliability is certainly high enough to make the RIRS score usable in research with groups.

As interesting as the short term reliability, is the evidence that the characteristic measured by RIRS has stability over long periods of time. Nettie Ledwith (1959) has followed a group of children from age six to age seventeen, administering Rorschach tests every year to age eleven to almost all of her sample, and testing about half of her group at ages thirteen, fourteen and seventeen again. These data are particularly useful because the children were most carefully chosen to represent a stratified random sample of the Pittsburgh public school population, and because nearly 100 per cent of the original sample was followed through age eleven.

The correlations from year to year are presented separately for

TABLE III

INTERCORRELATIONS OF RIRS SCORES FOR DIFFERENT AGES IN THE LEDWITH (1959) PITTSBURGH PUBLIC SCHOOL MALE POPULATION

Age	6	7	8	9	10	11	13	14	17
6		.36	.26	.22	.03	.25	.23	.05	.24
7			.55	.74	.34	.31	.47	.57	.58
8				.49	.79	.51	.53	.60	.48
9					.46	.59	.74	.74	.61
10						.64	.80	.68	.63
11							.87	.64	.47
13								.78	.52
14									.72
Ns	69	69	69	69	69	69	38	22	27
Means	1.38	1.42	1.53	1.61	1.56	1.67	1.71	1.84	2.19
Sigmas	.44	.54	.58	.55	.58	.65	.71	.69	.81

p values for	N	*p.05*	*p.01*
	70	.232	.302
	40	.304	.393
	35	.325	.418
	30	.349	.449
	27	.367	.470
	20	.423	.537

boys and girls in Tables III and IV. There are no sex differences. The correlations of age six with subsequent ages, although significant in many instances, are not high. From seven years of age on, in both boys and girls, the test-retest reliabilities from year to year, and even over a period of ten years, jump dramatically. For adjacent testings, with intertest intervals ranging from one to three years, the median reliability coefficient is .67. For test-retest intervals ranging from four to ten years, the median reliability coefficient is .60.

TABLE IV

INTERCORRELATIONS OF RIRS SCORES FOR DIFFERENT AGES IN THE
LEDWITH (1959) PITTSBURGH PUBLIC SCHOOL FEMALE POPULATION

Age	6	7	8	9	10	11	13	14	17
6		.29	.29	.17	.27	.19	.20	.04	.07
7			.57	.53	.63	.62	.45	.53	.59
8				.64	.57	.48	.44	.42	.44
9					.62	.72	.55	.74	.84
10						.97	.78	.62	.76
11							.85	.74	.80
13								.70	.83
14									.71
Ns	70	70	70	70	70	67	39	27	33
Means	1.61	1.40	1.55	1.70	1.69	1.64	1.78	1.84	2.03
Sigmas	.74	.65	.61	.60	.93	.81	.96	.69	1.12

p values for	N	p.05	p.01
	70	.232	.302
	40	.304	.393
	35	.325	.418
	30	.349	.449
	27	.367	.470

Similar evidence of long term reliability for the RIRS score
is found in the data obtained by Paulsen (1954). Paulsen re-
examined thirty normal children at two year intervals from average age seven to average age twelve. Her group was exceptionally
homogenous for intellectual ability, for cultural background, and
the group produced an exceptionally constricted set of Rorschach
records, but even in this group a correlation as high as .50 was
found for RIRS scores after a period of seven years (see Table V).

TABLE V

INTERCORRELATIONS[a] FOR 30 NORMAL CHILDREN OF RORSCHA6HS
TAKEN AT TWO YEAR INTERVALS

(Paulsen, 1954)

		Ages		
	6–8	8–10	10–12	12–14
Ages 6–8		.39	.09	.50
8–10			.25	.33
10–12				.18

[a] For N = 30, a correlation of .34 is significant at the .05 level, two tailed test.

It is possible that the long term reliability coefficients found in
the Ledwith and Paulsen samples are due to the fact that the
tests were repeated many times on each child, and the children
gave identical responses. If this were true, individuals would not
only have to see the same percept, but report it in very identical
language each time. It is only necessary to look at the systematic
increases in score with age (see Ch. VII) to realize that the
practice effect explanation is inadequate.

We have had the opportunity to score the basic protocols for the Gesell Institute studies of children and adolescents (Ames *et al.*, 1952; 1959). Many of the children they used were reexamined. We were able to find several small groups of five to nine children who had been tested and then retested again one year later. In nine such groups, retested after one year in the age range eight to fifteen, the retest coefficients (rhos) ranged from .00 to .78, the median value being .64. These subjects came from rather different socio-economic backgrounds than did the Ledwith and Paulsen children, and the type of test administration was also somewhat different. Examiners in the Ames group tended to press for responses more freely during the body of the test than did either of the other examiners.

These retest correlations are consistent in several samples differing widely in their characteristics. Significant correlations appear despite the rather marked intellectual and emotional changes accompanying growth and development from childhood to adolescence. These correlations show that we are dealing with a reasonably enduring style of response, a style which apparently becomes characteristic of a child at about age seven.

VARIATIONS IN INK BLOT TEST AND MODES OF ADMINISTRATION

In addition to various attempts to devise alternate sets of inkblots for the original Rorschach plates, there have been attempts to modify the form of administration of the test. Harrower and Steiner (1945) adapted the Rorschach blots for group administration, and more recently, Harrower (1959) has been experimenting with a self administering technique in which the subjects write their answers directly on a facsimile of the inkblots. Other inkblots have also been developed. One of the most promising of these new series is the forty-five card test described by Holtzman and his associates (1961) in which only one response per card is requested. Each variation in stimulus and each variation in procedure may contribute something different to Rorschach testing, and if alternate forms or alternate techniques for administration are to be used meaningfully, it is important to know what the deviation from the traditional technique introduces.

We have had the opportunity to study the effects on RIRS

scores of different inkblots and different techniques for administering the inkblots. These studies have shown that the magnitude of the RIRS score is dependent upon inkblots, and upon the mode of administration of the test. Although scores derived from different inkblots or techniques of administration correlate reasonably well, the means and the distributions of the scores will be affected. Table VI summarizes the data.

TABLE VI

SOME DIFFERENCES IN RIRS SCORES RELATED TO DIFFERENCES IN
INKBLOTS AND DIFFERENCES IN FORM OF ADMINISTRATION

1. Adolescent Emotionally Disturbed: Test repeated after three months; males and females, (N = 16)

	Behn Blots	Ror. Blots	Test	p
Mean	1.40	2.05	t = 2.50	.02
SD	.61	.84		

2. College Females, N = 12 in each group:

	Behn Blots	Ror. Blots	Test	p
Mean	1.23	1.66	U = 35	.05

3. Student Nurses, (N = 68): repeated examination after one week.

	Group Admin.	Individual	Test	p
Mean	3.09	2.21	t = 6.28	.0001
SD	.94	.74		

4. Ministers (N = 22): repeated examination, same day.

	Self Admin. Harrower Blots	Self Admin. Ror. Blots	Test	p
Mean	2.97	3.26	t	NS
SD	2.29	1.94		

5. College Students: group administered Holtzman blots.

	Males (N = 48)	Females (N = 44)
Median	2.11	2.25
Interquartile Range	1.68 – 2.56	1.75 – 2.87
Range	1.08 – 3.61	1.30 – 3.50

Behn Blots

In one sample of emotionally disturbed adolescents, the Rorschach tests were administered first, as part of the usual diagnostic battery; the Behn blots were administered for purposes of a reliability study some three months later. A *t* test for correlated means showed the two procedures produced significantly different scores. The RIRS scores using the Behn blots were significantly lower than the scores using the regular Rorschach plates. This result suggests that the Behn blots produce lower RIRS scores. However, the Behn blots were always administered second, and the subjects were called in specially to take the tests. The subjects' attitudes may have differed from first to second testing.

Schwartz and Kates (1957) had administered Rorschach and Behn blots in the "pre" portion of a study of the effects of psychological stress on inkblot responses. One group of twelve college girls received the Behn blots with standard instructions and the other group of twelve took the usual Rorschach test. A *U* test shows the two groups differed significantly. The Behn blots again produce records with lower scores than the Rorschach blots.

It is interesting to speculate about those features of the inkblots which might contribute to differences in response. Subjectively, the Behn blots have a more cramped appearance than the Rorschach plates. Perhaps the perceptual configuration of the forms themselves tend to restrict imaginative flow by virtue of presenting a "constricted" visual quality. There might be some interest in attempting to vary this type of perceptual quality of the inkblots systematically in order to discover something about the relationship between the perceptual and imaginative aspects of responses. As we indicate elsewhere in this chapter, there seem to be some differences among the Rorschach plates themselves in the degree to which they "pull" higher scores. It is not surprising that different inkblot series should also differ in their "pull."

Group Administration

Group administration is a common practice. Much of the large scale Rorschach testing has been accomplished by group techniques. There is considerable disagreement whether the same or different results are produced by the various group methods and by individual administration.

Half of Harrower & Steiner's (1945) student nurses took the individual form first and half took the group form first. The alternate method of administration followed one week later. The results show that group administration produces significantly higher RIRS scores than individual administration. The finding that group administration produces higher scores is borne out by a consideration of the results we have for a number of samples. (See Appendix listing distributions for various groups.) The median RIRS of distributions of scores for ten groups of adults who had taken the group Rorschach is about 2.88. The median RIRS of five distributions of scores of equally well educated adults who had taken the individual Rorschach is about 2.23. Moreover, the

ranges of scores tend to be broader among those who had taken
the group form of the test. The very highest scores tend to be
elicited by the group method of administration. This comparison
provides some further confirmation for the conclusion from the
one sample of student nurses that group records produce higher
scores than individual records.

Perhaps the fact that the group Rorschach calls upon written
responses is important. Osgood (1953) cites a number of studies
showing that written language is fuller and more varied in character than orally expressed language. Our results showing higher
scores for group Rorschachs may exemplify this principle in the
Rorschach situation. While one loses the behavioral observations
in the group tests, one might gain in the fullness of the verbal
material.

Harrower Blots

Harrower (1959) has developed a self administering form of
the inkblot test in which the subject writes his responses directly
on a facsimile of the inkblots. For this procedure she has used
reproductions of the Harrower blots. She also has attempted to
have subjects take the usual Rorschach test by mail. This procedure is very much analogous to the group method of administration, except that the subject is not limited by any time restric-
tion, and he holds the inkblot at close view instead of looking at
an enlarged version of it at a distance. The subject writes his
responses on answer forms while looking at the usual cards.

Data for twenty-two ministers who took both forms of the
test the same day were available to us. In this instance there
were no significant differences between the two procedures. Using a self administering procedure, the Harrower blots and the
Rorschach blots produce about the same level of richness of responses, as measured by RIRS. We have no information concerning the equivalence of the two sets of inkblots when other techniques of administration are employed. The mean scores are high,
generally speaking. Perhaps this is another instance where the
written record is a rich one.

Holtzman Inkblots

We have also had the opportunity to score a set of group

administered records using the Holtzman inkblots. Young (1959) administered forty blots in the Holtzman series and the subject was requested to give but one response for each card. The records were administered by Young in a large classroom to students attending a summer session. These students are somewhat more heterogenous in age, intelligence and experience than students attending the regular session. There were no other records available for comparison on these same subjects.

The median values for males and females are similar to the values obtained for other groups. The *range* of scores in both males and females is somewhat more restricted than we are accustomed to find in group Rorschachs in college populations. It is possible that the form upon which the responses were written is responsible for the restricted range of scores. The form left a comparatively small amount of space for the response proper since a great deal of the response page was devoted to a reproduction of the inkblot itself, for purposes of establishing location. It is possible that the absolute RIRS score for any set of blots will be affected by such an essentially extraneous condition.

Interpretation of Data Relating to Alternate Forms of Administration

Jensen (1959) has stated three criteria a parallel form of a test must meet if it is to be considered truly a parallel form. The alternate form must yield the same mean and the same standard deviation as the original test, and it must correlate with the original test as highly as the original test correlates with itself. According to these criteria, our results suggest that the Behn and the group administered form of the Rorschach do not constitute parallel forms for RIRS. When the same form of the inkblots is administered twice in the same way reliability coefficients vary around .88. Correlations between different forms are in the neighborhood of .70. Considering the difference in mean scores reported above between the Behn and the Rorschach, and between individual and group administered forms, we conclude that the variations in procedure do not provide precisely parallel forms, in so far as the RIRS score is concerned. Separate norms should be developed for different types of blots and for different forms of administration.

ANALYSIS OF CARD PULL

One of the important considerations in Rorschach testing is the issue of stimulus quality. The Rorschach cards have structure, but are ambiguous. There are popular responses, and "good form" responses, conforming to stimulus characteristics. Some cards are more likely to produce shading responses, some color responses, some movement responses, and some are much more likely to be rejected than others. On some, W responses are produced frequently, and on others, D responses predominate. These phenomena are well known.

Card pull, or stimulus value, takes on important meaning in at least two ways. If we are interested in analyzing the sequence of the subject's responses, as a feature of his personality, we must have some expectation of what he is most likely to produce on any given card. Secondly, if we are interested in the variability of his response, we must have some idea how much is contributed by the properties of the inkblots themselves. We undertook this kind of an analysis after we had studied a number of different groups of cases. The description of the groups and the number of cases in each group may be found in Table VII.

All of these people had been tested individually using the standard Rorschach inkblots. This analysis used only the first response to each card for each subject. We then obtained a mean for each card for each group, and we used these means as the values for analysis. Since we were interested in whether the various groups ordered the cards in a similar manner, we chose to treat the means as equivalent from group to group despite different Ns. For each group, the cards were ranked from one to ten according to the magnitude of the mean RIRS score for that card for that group. These ranks were then analyzed according to the method described by Kramer (1956) and by a concordance analysis (Siegel, 1956).

Kramer's method of analysis for multiple comparisons permits one to treat the various cards as "treatments," and the various groups as "replicates." The sum of ranks for each card shows that the cards are ordered from low RIRS score to high RIRS score in this fashion: V, I, VI, IV, VIII, X, II, IX, III, VII. Cards III and VII pull RIRS scores which are significantly high ($p =$ .05 or less), while Cards V, I and VI pull RIRS scores which are

TABLE VII

GROUPS OF CASES AND NUMBERS STUDIED FOR CARD PULL

Group	N
Emotionally Disturbed Adolescents Unselected sample	24
Emotionally Disturbed Adolescents Used in test-retest study	15
Emotionally Disturbed Adolescents Performance IQ 15 points higher than verbal	29
Emotionally Disturbed Adolescents Verbal IQ 15 points higher than performance	24
Text-book obsessive compulsives	8
Text-book hysterics	8
Veterans Administration Psychoneurotics	19
College Students Volunteers in sensory deprivation study	15
Executives—Superior Normals	20

significantly low ($p = .05$ or less). Cards III and VII are significantly different from cards V, I, and VI, but not from all others. Cards V, I and VI are not statistically different from the remaining five cards.

There is definitely a card pull. Suggestively III and VII yield high RIRS scores because movement is so frequent on these cards. The popular "bat" on V may contribute to its low value; I yielding low scores might be suggestive of some initial "shock"; and low scores on VI may be suggestive of repression due to "sex shock," as is sometimes suggested.

The concordance analysis from these same data yielded a W of .29, significant at well below $p = .01$. This suggests there is some degree of agreement in the way in which the various groups order the set of ten cards. While the agreement is statistically significant, the degree of agreement is far from perfect. For example, while Card V generally pulled low RIRS scores, for two of the groups it ranked 9th and 10th highest. Card VI had ranks ranging from 2nd through 8th and Card I from 1st through 9th. Cards III and VII generally pulled high scores. For these two cards, the range of ranks was considerably narrower (5th through 10th). Of course, when we deal with individual cases, the scores tend to be quite variable. Few individuals actually approximate the ordering of cards as given by the means for the group.

While one must be cautious about sequence interpretations,

and not attribute psychodynamic significance to variations in performance which may be a function of the stimulus properties of the cards, these data leave room to consider the meaningfulness of individual sequences of RIRS scores. In another chapter, we give some examples of sequence analysis of the scores which we feel are justified, despite reservations which might follow from an analysis such as this.

VARIATIONS IN SET AND EMOTIONAL CLIMATE DURING TESTING

Rorschach himself conducted some experiments to determine the extent to which conscious effort could alter performance, and in recent years there has been increasing interest in the influence of various sets, and the emotional climate of the testing situation. Zax, Stricker, and Weiss (1960) have reviewed this literature and suggested some scoring variables remain stable, while others are unstable. A full discussion of the problems in this area is provided by these authors.

Since set and the emotional climate of the testing situation have been shown to be effective in altering some aspects of Rorschach performance, it was felt advisable to study the influence of some of these variables on RIRS. We have not been able to study these factors systematically, but we have had the opportunity to test the effects of several different variables on RIRS.

Status and Sex of Examiner

Campbell and Fiddleman (1959) studied the effect of the examiner's status upon Rorschach responses. The status of the examiner in the subjects' eyes was varied by introducing the examiner as Dr. S, a "research scientist" or Mr. S, "a student working on a term paper." There was one male examiner and one female examiner, but all of the eighty-four subjects were males. Analysis of RIRS scores for these data indicated no significant source of variance for examiners, no significant source for status set, and no significant interactions.

While there was no significant effect of status set on the RIRS score, Campbell and Fiddleman did find the status set was effective in influencing the response total (R). Their results show the set they used was effective in influencing one important aspect of performance, but the particular status set did not have any influence on the RIRS score. Campbell and Fiddleman also reported no significant examiner effect for other Rorschach variables in this study.

Sleep Deprivation

Loveland and Singer (1959) studied sleep deprivation in twenty-five army volunteers. The men were subjected to ninety-eight hours of sleep deprivation. They were tested initially, after some eighty hours of wakefulness and after having had normal sleep for three days to "recover." Another group of twenty-five men lived under identical conditions for a week, were subjected to the same tests at the same time intervals, but they were not deprived of sleep. These records were rescored for RIRS.

Control subjects showed no significant differences between the three testings. (The reliability coefficients are reported in another section.) Subjects who had been deprived of sleep showed no significant change from the baseline condition, following sleep deprivation. However, nineteen of twenty-five subjects showed a slight decrease in RIRS at the third testing, following recovery from sleep deprivation. The median baseline score was 1.63, while the median score for the third examination, following recovery, was 1.53. This difference is significant at $p < .01$ by Wilcoxon's signed rank test, but the actual magnitude of the change is quite trivial.

Loveland and Singer concluded that sleep deprivation results in very little change in the personality structure as measured by changes in the Rorschach and three other projective tests. The analysis of the Rorschachs for RIRS would lead to much the same conclusion. Sleep deprivation apparently does not seriously affect the RIRS scores, although it is a sufficiently intensive stressor to produce hallucinatory phenomena in some subjects.

Stress by Self Esteem Threat ·

Various investigations have considered the effects of experimentally induced stress or anxiety upon performance. Rorschach performance has been shown to be sensitive to stress and anxiety, induced in various ways. Schwartz and Kates (1957) examined two groups of female college students, selected from the upper and lower 20 per cent of the distribution of the Taylor Manifest Anxiety Scale. These individuals were tested twice, within two weeks, using the Behn and Rorschach tests in counterbalanced sequence. Just before the second testing, half of the Ss in each group were given a typewritten personality evaluation, supposedly based on the first inkblot administration, which advised they were poorly adjusted. They were then given the second test. The control group, matched to the experimental Ss for the initial psychogram, was simply reexamined. On the basis of differences in the usual Rorschach scores, Schwartz and Kates concluded there were significant differences between high and low anxiety Ss, as defined by the MAS, and that the type of stress employed resulted in changes on the Rorschach which imply behavioral constriction.

Schwartz and Kates' (1957) records were rescored blindly for RIRS. An analysis of variance for the pre scores only revealed a significant difference ($p = .03$) between the Behn and the Rorschach tests, the Rorschach test yielding the less repressed scores, as we have found elsewhere with different groups. The groups which eventually became experimental and controls did not differ significantly. There was a difference between the high and low MAS groups which was significant at about $p = .10$. The low MAS group tended to have the less repressed scores.

An analysis of variance of the RIRS difference scores, pre and post stress, revealed a significant interaction of stress with MAS. Stress resulted in a drop in the RIRS scores (increased

TABLE VIII

MEAN RIRS SCORES BEFORE AND AFTER STRESS

		Pre	Post
Hi MAS	Stress	1.29	1.26
	Control	1.32	1.40
Lo MAS	Stress	1.64	.99
	Control	1.54	1.64

repression), and the change was much greater for the low MAS group than for the high MAS group. These results are consistent with Schwartz and Kates' conclusion that "self esteem" stress results in behavioral constriction, as measured by other aspects of Rorschach performance. Schwartz and Kates did not find any significant interaction between stress and MAS standing.

The RIRS score elicited one result (i.e., the interaction of stress with MAS scores) different from an analysis of the usual Rorschach scores, but findings using the RIRS score also led to conclusions paralleling those from other data. RIRS may be sensitive to variables not reflected in other aspects of Rorschach performance. These results suggest that RIRS may be influenced by "self esteem" stress, and that the influence is in the direction of producing a more repressed score. It is also worth noting that a significant correlation between pre and post tests was produced in both the experimental and control groups, despite the fact that there was a significant effect of stress upon the *mean* RIRS score (see Table II).

Hypnotically Induced Anxiety

When one tells a subject he is maladjusted, it is assumed that the subject experiences "anxiety," and that subsequent behavior should reflect the subject's response to his anxious state. If "anxiety" can be induced by other means, will the effects on Rorschach performance remain constant? Working with medical and nursing student volunteers, Levitt and Grosz (1960) induced anxiety by means of a hypnotic suggestion. Three records were obtained from each S on the same day. The first was taken in a hypnotic state without special suggestion, the second in a hypnotically induced anxiety state, and the third in the normal waking state. A post-hypnotic suggestion was given to make each S amnesic for the Rorschach test after each of the first two administrations. A "diffuse, non-specific anxiety" was induced in each S by a psychiatrist using a detailed suggestion in which the words "anxiety," "fear," "apprehension," and "panic" were used. All Ss verbalized feelings of anxiety, and all Ss showed some of the physical manifestations commonly associated with anxiety.

The records for each of the Ss in the waking, hypnotic and hypnotically induced anxiety state were scored for RIRS. The mean RIRS scores were 3.15 for the waking state, 3.01 for the hypnotic state, and 4.22 for the hypnotically induced anxiety state. The F value for 2 and 22 degrees of freedom is 4.32, $p < .01$. The t test showed that the hypnotically induced anxiety state differed significantly from both the waking and the hypnotic state, but the waking and hypnotic state did not differ from each other significantly. The conclusions parallel Levitt and Grosz's conclusions working from the usual Rorschach scores in that they also concluded that only the hypnotically induced anxiety state led to any significant change in Rorschach performance.

On the surface, these results are directly opposite to the findings obtained when anxiety was induced by a self esteem threat. There, RIRS scores showed greater repression. Now when anxiety is induced by the hypnotic suggestion, the RIRS score shows considerably reduced repression. It is apparent that the hypnotic anxiety state has different consequences than the self esteem threat induced anxiety state.

Levitt and Grosz (1960) have argued that most laboratory techniques for inducing anxiety are of questionable efficacy, and they therefore used an hypnotically induced anxiety state. When these apparently contradictory results were discussed with Levitt in correspondence, he suggested that when anxiety is low, repression is operative, and is successful. If the anxiety level is high, it may be an indication of the failure of defenses. The increase in RIRS score would then reflect the intensity of the anxiety, and the failure of defense. By implication, the Schwartz and Kates procedure produced less anxiety than the hypnosis did. Presumably the level of anxiety was sufficiently low so that repressive defenses could manage it.

Set Given by Instructions

An alternative, and more parsimonious hypothesis suggests that the two situations differ in the task demands and in the *implicit* instructions involved in the procedures.

Schwartz and Kates Ss were told a previous Rorschach test (the pre-test) showed they were poorly adjusted, and that the purpose of the present examination (the post-test) was to check this finding. While these instructions probably caused S distress, and probably induced "anxiety," one can reason that it would be to S's advantage in the situation to conceal as much as he could from the examiner, while still responding to the test in the re-examination. The increased "behavioral constriction" Schwartz and Kates found in the "threatened" group might well have reflected an implicit set to *conceal* aroused in the testing situation.

Levitt and Grosz's Ss were hypnotized, and in accepting the

hypnotist's suggestion to feel anxious, it seems reasonable to believe these Ss would follow through during testing by showing themselves to be in a state of anxiety. Where Schwartz and Kates' Ss were set to *"conceal,"* Levitt and Grosz's Ss were set to *"reveal."* Apparently contradictory RIRS results between the two studies may possibly be explained by the difference in response set which was produced by differences in the implicit instructions of the two testing situations. If true, one should be able to produce the results of the two studies by giving explicit instructions to recreate the implicit instruction which may have been operative in the two studies. If the hypothesis is valid, then explicit instructions to "reveal" anxiety should produce a comparatively unrepressed record, while instructions to "conceal" anxiety should produce more constricted records.

We undertook a study to test this hypothesis, in collaboration with Anthony Graziano, at the University of Bridgeport. Male and female undergraduate psychology students served as Ss. A task oriented set was first established with each S, instructions essentially informing S that he was going to be asked to respond to ink blots as though he were a certain kind of person. Following this he was asked to assume, in sequence, three "roles" in responding to the Rorschach ink blots. In one role he was to respond as himself:

> This time I want you to just be yourself. I am going to show you the cards one at a time. I want you to look at each one and tell me everything you see in the cards and everything they remind you of.

In another role S was to respond as though he were an anxious person:

> This time I want you to respond to the ink blots as though you are a very anxious, scared, tense, apprehensive, panicky individual. You are afraid that you are becoming very emotionally disturbed. You have come to me on your own, seeking help, and you want to cooperate and let me know as much as possible about yourself so that I might help you. Look at each card and tell me everything you see in each card and everything it reminds you of. Remember, you are

disturbed and you want to let me know as much as possible about yourself through your responses to the inkblots.

A third role instructed S to respond as though he were an anxious person trying to hide the fact he is anxious:

> This time I want you to respond to the inkblots as though you were a very anxious, scared, tense, apprehensive, panicky individual. You are frightened that you are becoming very emotionally disturbed. You are being tested and you have to cooperate with the test but you want to hide your disturbance from me and you want to appear as normal as possible. Look at each card and tell me everything you see in each card and everything it reminds you of. Remember, you feel disturbed inside yourself but you want to hide your disturbance from me and you want to appear as normal as possible.

Two Rorschach cards were used for each "role" and the "card" effects and order of "roles" controlled.

Table IX presents the results. The data were analyzed by

TABLE IX

MEDIAN RIRS SCORES FOR "BE YOURSELF," "SHOW ANXIETY" AND
"CONCEAL ANXIETY" INSTRUCTIONS, IN MALES AND FEMALES

	A Be Yourself		B Show Anxiety		C Conceal Anxiety	
	Median	Range	Median	Range	Median	Range
Males (N = 18)	2.60	.60–20.00	5.09[a]	1.57–11.33	3.08	1.20–20.50
Females (N = 18)	2.87	1.50–12.00	5.67[b]	2.00–23.50	3.25	1.25–10.50

[a] B differs significantly ($p < .01$) by Kramer's (1956) analysis of variance by ranks from A, but not from C instruction. C does not differ significantly from A.

[b] B differs significantly ($p < .01$) from both A and C instruction. C does not differ significantly from A.

means of Kramer's analysis of variance by ranks (Kramer, 1956). This analysis was carried out separately in the males and females. Among the males, the "show anxiety" condition resulted in significantly less repressed ($p = .01$) scores than the "be yourself" condition, but there was no significant difference between the "conceal anxiety" and "be yourself" conditions. Among the females, the "show anxiety" condition produced significantly ($p = .01$) less repressed records than both the other conditions, but the "be yourself" and the "conceal anxiety" instructions did not result in any significant difference. The hypothesis that the set S had would result in systematic changes in the RIRS score is thus partially confirmed.

We originally expected the "conceal" instructions would result in scores below the baseline of "be yourself." This expectation was not borne out. If anything, the "conceal anxiety" instructions led to a slight though not significant increase in RIRS, or a decrease in repression. Examination of the records suggests that many of the Ss responded to the "anxiety" portion of the instruction and produced similar content irrespective of the instruction. It is possible that had we not used the term "anxiety" in the initial instruction, but just the set to be as "normal as possible," the predicted decrease in RIRS might have resulted.

The RIRS score has been shown to be quite reliable under a variety of circumstances. In these three studies, despite the fact that the instructions resulted in systematic changes in the mean RIRS score, significant correlations between conditions were still obtained. In the Schwartz and Kates data, the reliability coefficient (rho) was .50 in both the stress and control groups. It must be remembered that two weeks intervened between examinations and that Behn and Rorschach blots were used. Both the reliability coefficients are significant at $p = .05$, for N = 12. In the Levitt and Grosz data, the correlation (rho) between the waking and hypnotic state was .38 (not significant), between the hypnotic and the hypnotically induced anxiety state .51 ($p = .05$), and between the waking state and the hypnotically induced state .78 ($p < .01$). The Ns in each instance are 12.

The present data consisted of the mean score for responses given to three pairs of cards, one pair used in each condition. The Kendall's W for the three conditions was .72 in the males, and in the females, .75. Both values are significant well below the .01 level of confidence and both indicate substantial agreement in the ordering of the Ss, despite the fact that the different conditions resulted in significant mean changes in RIRS.

RIRS increased with instructions to show anxiety because the score weights adjectives and verbs heavily. If more terms indicating subjective disturbance are produced, then the index of repression score increases. What is most interesting however, is the finding that the Ss maintained their relative rank orders very well even when the mean for the condition changes. The RIRS score is responsive to changed conditions, but Ss who produce high scores under one condition will produce even higher scores under a stimulating circumstance. Ss who tend to give repressed records under normal circumstances will continue to produce relatively repressed records under stimulating conditions. The response style measured by RIRS is relatively consistent then, as we have shown in other reliability studies.

If the conditions of administration are constant, and on re-test S's RIRS score changes in either direction, one must consider the possibility that his attitude toward the testing situation has changed. With an increased RIRS score on reexamination, S may be more willing to reveal various aspects of himself. With decreased RIRS, one might adopt the hypothesis that S is taking the test with greater constraint. The RIRS score may provide a useful quantification of this aspect of S's test taking attitudes.

SUMMARY OF RELIABILITY STUDIES

Our studies of reliability have produced rather extensive data which help to elucidate the properties of RIRS. The data may also have some bearing on problems related to the Rorschach method itself, since RIRS deals very directly with details of verbalization, so important to the clinical interpretation of the protocol.

First, we have shown that RIRS can be scored with considerable consistency by different scorers working with different types of raw data (individual records, group records, different ink-blots). Since RIRS is designed to quantify features of the response which are generally held to be qualitative in nature, the success of the scoring manual shows that qualitative aspects of responses can be quantified. Careful detailing of the properties of responses to which clinicians are sensitive can result in the necessary objectivity and communicability.

Second, while RIRS has been shown to be relatively stable, it is also sensitive to change at times when one would expect change. There appears to be developmental increment in the score and yet the correlations over periods of years show the Ss relative rank order in his own group is almost as stable as rank order in intellectual performance over similar periods of time. Klopfer *et al.* (1954) suggest "The Rorschach results would be suspect if they were identical or (highly similar) when major changes intervene between test and retest, or if no continuity were found between test and retest" (p. 447). The reliability data show RIRS measures a function which does show change and continuity. Over the short run, simple retest produces no significant changes in the scores. The correlation between testings is quite high, when the conditions of reexamination are constant.

RIRS is sensitive to changed conditions of administration, but the score does not shift for trivial reasons. One study has shown it is stable with different examiners, and a condition as intensive as sleep deprivation does not affect the score. On the other hand, techniques for inducing "anxiety" do cause the score to change, and have different effects on performance. Instructional sets can also induce marked changes in the level of the score. Despite the fact that some conditions of administration lead to changes in the mean level of RIRS scores, in practically every instance where the mean changed, the relative rank order of Ss remained reasonably constant.

RIRS may be quite useful in studies of the inkblots as stimuli, as in the analysis of "card pull," and in studies in which some measure of change in performance is desired. If the conditions of administration are constant, it is reasonable to believe that any sizable change in the score is due to some change in the subject.

In describing the background of RIRS, it has been suggested that Rorschach workers make use of much more than the formal scores in interpreting the test. The details of the way in which the responses are expressed are important data for the clinician working with an individual record. In one sense, RIRS may be considered a measure of the "raw material" available to the clinician for interpretation. The score is high when the responses are fully elaborated, and lower when the responses are less well developed verbally. The fact that at least this one measurable aspect of the "raw material" is reliable is important. The findings suggest that some of the response properties which provide cues for interpretations are stable. It may be stretching a point, but we feel that the data not only demonstrate the level of reliability of the particular score, but they also provide some small degree of justification for the clinical practice of dealing with the details of the way in which responses are expressed.

Chapter V

RIRS, RORSCHACH DETERMINANTS AND TAT "TRANSCENDENCE" MEASURES

RELATIONSHIP TO STANDARD RORSCHACH SCORES

In DEVELOPING ANY NEW MEASURE, it is useful to understand its relationship to the old. The old and the new may then be used together to clarify each other. Similarities and differences between methods of treating the same basic data may become apparent.

Scored Rorschach records were available from a number of different sources. All of the records were scored originally by the investigator who collected them. We did not attempt to rescore the records. The individual records had inquiries; location, determinant and content scores were based upon these inquiries. The RIRS scores were obtained without reference to the original scores. Since RIRS scores are based upon verbalizations in the free associations only, there is some difference in the basic data used by the two methods of scoring.

The first sample consisted of sixty-eight student nurses who had been administered individual tests. The records were obtained by Harrower-Erickson and Steiner (1945). Table X presents contingency coefficients showing the relationship between RIRS and the various Klopfer scoring components. One column presents coefficients based on raw scores and the other coefficients based on per cent scores.

The relationships seem highest with M, m, C', and experience balance. In general, subjects with a dilated experience balance give high RIRS scores, while Ss with a constricted experience balance give low RIRS scores. Subjects who produce a rich record by the usual Rorschach scoring criteria, tend to produce high RIRS scores. Richness in the verbalization tends to be accompanied by richness in the use of the various determinants.

TABLE X

CONTINGENCY COEFFICIENTS SHOWING THE RELATIONSHIP
BETWEEN RIRS AND THE USUAL RORSCHACH SCORES

Variable	Coefficient for Per Cent Score	p	Coefficient for Raw Score	p
R			.00	NS
W	.00	NS	.00	NS
D	.00	NS	.00	NS
d	.22	NS	.00	NS
Dds	.00	NS	.00	NS
M	.31	<.05	.38	<.05
FM	.00	NS	.18	NS
m	.24	NS	.31	.05
K	.00	NS	.00	NS
F	.24	NS	.00	NS
Fc	.22	NS	.35	<.05
C′	.32	.05	.28	<.10
FC	.00	NS	.00	NS
CF	.18	NS	.30	.05
Sum C	.22	NS	.28	<.10
M/Sum C (dilated)			.45	.01
Hd	.00	NS	.00	NS
A	.00	NS	.00	NS
Ad	.28	.10	.30	.05
P	.00	NS	.00	NS
O	.00	NS	.23	NS

We also investigated the relationship of RIRS to some of the scores on the Holtzman ink blots. Two sets of records were available. One was for college males ($N = 48$) and one for college females ($N = 44$). The records were collected and scored by Young (1959) who scored the records partly by Holtzman's system and partly by standard scoring techniques. He used a group method of administration. Table XI shows the relationship of RIRS to scores on the Holtzman test. Since the Holtzman test

TABLE XI

RANK ORDER COEFFICIENTS SHOWING THE RELATIONSHIP BETWEEN
RIRS AND THE RORSCHACH TYPE SCORES IN THE HOLTZMAN BLOTS

Variable	Males (N = 48)	p	Females (N = 44)	p
W	.43	<.01	.35	<.01
M	.74	<.01	.74	<.01
FM	.51	<.01	.52	<.01
m	.07	NS	.38	<.01
Movement energy level	.70	<.01	.74	<.01
F	−.45	<.01	−.45	<.01
FC	.24	<.10	.45	<.01
CF	.27	<.10	.19	NS
M/ΣC (dilated)	.40	<.01	.26	<.10
Sh (Σof ratings)	.30	<.05	.20	NS
Anatomy	.27	<.10	−.26	<.10
P	.21	>.10	.06	NS

holds *R* constant by requiring one response per card, raw scores were used in the correlations. Correlations were obtained only for those variables shown in the table. Scores peculiar to the Holtzman test such as Form Definiteness or Form Appropriateness were not correlated with RIRS. The content scales such as Pathognomic Verbalization, Anxiety, Hostility, Barrier and Penetration were not scored by Young and were thus not examined.

Once again, in this sample, the relationship with various types of movement responses is quite high. The significant negative correlation with the number of pure form responses (F), and the correlation with a measure of the experience balance support the previous conclusion that fullness in the verbalization of the response is accompanied by the use of a variety of determinants.

The correlations with the movement responses *M* and *FM* are particularly high, and the correlation with *M* was highest in the individual Rorschachs as well. The high correlations may very well be an artifact since movement responses are typically expressed in verbs and verbs enter into the index of repression score. It seemed advisable, however, to explore whether there was a relationship between *M* and the index of repression when the index was computed independently of the use of verbs, since *M* is a critical Rorschach variable about which much is known.

A large number of records were available to us from various sources.* For purposes of this study, we used six different samples:

1. *Normal Adolescents:* A group of twenty records of normal adolescents were collected as part of a validation study of the index of repression. The Ss were all male, and were tested at a local, suburban high school. They were assigned to the study by the guidance counselor of the school. The records were individually administered, using standard instructions and using the Rorschach blots.

2. *College Females:* Holzman and Gardner (1959) reported a study of the Rorschach records of extreme levelers and ex-

---

* Much of what follows is taken from an article which appeared in the *Journal of Projective Techniques* (1962, 26:299-304), and the material is used with permission of the publishers.

treme sharpeners. The twenty Ss were female university students, ranging in age from eighteen to twenty-one. The Ss were selected from a larger group of eighty on the basis of their performances in the Schematizing Test. The Rorschachs were individually administered using standard blots and instructions.

3. *Student Nurses:* In the standardization of the group Rorschach test, Harrower-Erickson and Steiner (1945) collected individual Rorschach records from sixty-eight student nurses who were also administered the group Rorschach. Half the Ss received the group test first, and half received the individual test first. Retest took place about a week later. Standard blots and standard instructions were used. The data reported here are based upon the individual records.

4. *College Females:* These records were collected by Page (1957) as part of a study of daydreamers. Half the thirty-five Ss admitted to a great deal of daydreaming, while the other half were low scorers on Page's daydreaming scale. The records were administered in group following Harrower-Erickson and Steiner's procedure.

5. *College Females, Holtzman Inkblots:* These forty-four records were collected by Young (1959) as part of a study of Witkin's field dependence hypothesis. The group version of the Holtzman inkblot test (1961) was administered following Holtzman's procedure. The Ss were female undergraduates attending a summer session.

6. *College Males, Holtzman Inkblots:* These records were also collected by Young (1959). The forty-eight Ss were male undergraduates attending a summer session. These records, and the ones described above are the same as those used in a study of the relationship to the usual scoring categories.

Because we were interested in the relationship of the index of repression to M, and verbs are part of the index of repression score, the index of repression was computed for each S, omitting any scoring for verbs. This includes human, animal and inanimate movement. At the same time, count was kept of the number of scorable verbs used spontaneously by the S (see manual for rules for scoring verbs). The Ms were scored by those who took the original records.

TABLE XII

THE CORRELATION BETWEEN *M* AS USUALLY SCORED AND RIRS
COMPUTED WITHOUT CONSIDERING VERBS

Sample Individual Rorschachs	N	r	p
Male adolescents	20	.59	<.01
College females (Holzman and Gardner, 1959)	20	.41	.08
Female student nurses (Harrower-Erickson and Steiner, 1945)	68	.28	.04
Group Rorschachs			
College females (Page, 1957)	35	.21	NS
College females, Holtzman inkblots (Young, 1959)	44	.63	<.01
College males, Holtzman inkblots (Young, 1959)	48	.76	<.01

Table XII summarizes the relationship between *M* as usually scored, and the index of repression score computed without verbs. In general, the results are consistent in showing a positive relationship between the index of repression score without verbs, and the *M* response as usually scored. The correlations using the Holtzman blots may be better because of the greater reliability of scores based upon the written output to forty cards.

The index of repression is a mean, and it controls the factor of response total. Our previous work has shown that *R* is uncorrelated with the repression index. The significant correlations between *M* and the index of repression are not based upon any common dependence of both scores on *R*. However, as a further check, a contingency coefficient was obtained between *M%* and the index of repression score computed without verbs, using Harrower's sample. The relationship was significant, and the contingency coefficient using *M* was exactly the same as the coefficient using *M%*, .38 in both cases.

Table XIII summarizes the correlations between the total number of verbs scored and the index of repression score computed without reference to verbs. The correlations are uniformly significant, and fall within a relatively narrow range. It is clear that Ss who produce more verbs also produce fuller responses in other respects. Ss who produce many verbs also exhibit other qualities of verbalization that raise the RIRS score.

Does the relationship of RIRS to the fullness of the Rorschach protocol merely reflect a characteristic verbosity? It is probably true that people who "emit" a lot of words during Rorschach free

TABLE XIII

THE CORRELATION BETWEEN THE TOTAL VERB SCORE AND RIRS
COMPUTED WITHOUT CONSIDERING VERBS

Sample Individual Rorschachs	N	r	p
Male adolescents	20	.59	< .01
College females (Holzman and Gardner, 1959)	20	.63	< .01
Female student nurses (Harrower-Erickson and Steiner, 1945)	68	.35	< .01
Group Rorschachs			
College females (Page, 1957)	35	.43	.02
College females, Holtzman inkblots (Young, 1959)	44	.69	< .01
College males, Holtzman inkblots (Young, 1959)	48	.62	< .01

associations will tend to get higher RIRS scores than those who do not. But if characteristic verbosity is the issue, then RIRS scores should be related to total verbal output in another testing situation.

Page (1957) administered TATs to the same sample from whom Rorschachs were obtained. We found no relationship between the total number of words S produced on the TAT and RIRS.

RELATIONSHIP TO TAT "TRANSCENDENCE" SCORES

Singer and Herman (1954) and Singer, Wilensky and Mc-Craven (1956) have shown that TAT transcendence scores correlate with Rorschach M. The transcendence score is based upon the degree to which Ss' descriptions of the TAT cards introduce material which goes beyond card description. The transcendence score, devised originally by Weisskopf (1950), seems to have much in common with RIRS in that both scores seem to measure the degree to which S introduces material beyond that given by the qualities of the stimulus. Since M relates to RIRS, and RIRS and transcendence scores have much in common in their approach, we thought it was worth looking at this aspect of TAT stories.

TATs which had been administered in such fashion as to yield transcendence scores were not available to us. However, Page (1956) had developed a "level of interpretation" rating for TATs which seemed to have something in common with the transcendence index. Page had rated his TATs on an eight point scale ranging from "rejection" and "description of physical appearance" to "complete narrative with interpretation of feelings, attitudes and/or thoughts of characters." A score for each S was based upon the mean rating for six TAT cards. The correlation between the full index of repression score and the mean "level of interpretation" rating was .35,* significant at $p = .05$ for N = 35. Apparently the issue is *how* it is said, and not *how much* is said.

Rorschachs and TATs were available for two groups of children who had been studied by Witkin (Personal communication). The TATs had been rated for *organizational level* on a four point scale. *Level one* is defined in this manner: "Protocols to be scored as having no organization at all are, in a literal sense, not stories, but simply descriptions of objects, people and scenes, usually very briefly stated, with no attempt at interpretation of what is going on, or what some person in the picture is feeling." *Level four* stories: ". . . involve elaborate but consistent plots, or extensive consideration of inner motives of characters, or a high level of awareness and productive use of most of the outstanding features of the card, or the creation of characters not pictured on the card, who played important roles in the story."

This scale is similar to Page's level of interpretation scale and to Weisskopf's transcendence index. In one sample of thirty ten year old boys, the RIRS score correlated .65 with the TAT organization rating. This value is significant well below the .01 level of confidence. In the second sample of twenty-four ten year old boys, the RIRS score correlated .32 with the organization ratings. This correlation is significant at approximately the 10 per cent level of confidence. We cannot say that the scale Witkin's group used is the exact equivalent of the scale Page used, but the two scales seem to be getting at the same quality of TAT responses, and in all three samples the correlations with RIRS are significant, or are nearly significant.

---

* The correlation between M alone and the TAT "level of interpretation" was .10, a value which is not significant. Apparently the additional features of the index of repression beyond M add a significant component to the evaluation of Rorschach responses. These results are not directly comparable to Singer *et al.* (1954; 1956) because the technique of scoring "transcendence" differs considerably.

SUMMARY OF RORSCHACH DETERMINANTS AND TAT "TRANSCENDENCE" MEASURES

The correlations of the M scores with the index of repression score, and the correlations of the number of verbs with the index of repression score suggest the usefulness of dealing directly with the language of the responses. The M response is not totally unique in itself, but it seems to be part of a tendency to produce well defined, elaborated and individualized responses. The style of rich, verbal expression may be observed in responses other than those relatively few which happen to contain verbs. Sarason's (1954) opinion that subjective and internal factors may be evaluated just as well in any response, and not in M responses alone, receives some support from these findings.

The correlations of RIRS with M and with the transcendence type scores are also important because they amplify the interpretation of an RIRS score. The body of research relating M responses and transcendence scores to the ability to delay gratification of impulse (Singer, 1960) may be pertinent to our understanding of RIRS. These findings, in conjunction with the relationship between RIRS and dilated experience balance, suggest that high RIRS reflects a general richness of intellectual and affective responsiveness, and a readiness to experience one's inner "workings" and to respond accordingly. Moreover, since RIRS is a measure based directly on the language of the responses, a theory relating RIRS to the ability to delay gratification of impulse may make use of concepts important in the study of language. Specifically, the mediating function of language might be invoked in trying to understand the relationship between language behavior on the Rorschach test, and behavioral characteristics observed in a variety of other situations. In the final chapter on the interpretation of the RIRS score, we shall try to develop this conception more fully.

Chapter VI

RELATIONSHIP TO INTELLIGENCE AND ACHIEVEMENT

CORRELATIONS WITH IQ MEASURES

A FUNDAMENTAL QUESTION about any projective measure is the degree of its relationship to measures of intelligence. Such information is particularly important when one is dealing with measures which seem to be heavily dependent upon verbal skills. For example, if the measure is used as an independent variable in selecting Ss for further study, it may turn out that one has selected Ss who differ for intellectual ability, and all subsequent findings may reflect differences between groups selected for intelligence.

Table XIV presents the correlations of RIRS with a variety of measures of intelligence, in a number of different age groups, in both males and females. The correlation coefficients range from —.21 to + .66 with an overall median of about .21.* The correlations tend to be somewhat higher in female groups (median = .25) than in the male groups (median = .15), and in general the correlations with verbal tests seem to be somewhat higher than with nonverbal tests. Individual tests seem to yield somewhat higher correlations than group tests, but none of the differences are particularly striking. The level of correlation seems to be about the same whether we deal with adults or with children.

All in all, on the basis of thirteen independent samples and sixty-two correlations with different types of tests, and several factors of intelligence, we conclude that the correlation of the index of repression score with measures of intelligence is quite low, although there is undoubtedly a relationship. RIRS correlates

---

* This measure of central tendency of the set of correlations is a convenient way of summarizing the data. We do not feel that any more refined technique of averaging correlations is warranted or necessary in this context.

TABLE XIV

RIRS AND INTELLIGENCE

Sex	Age and Group	N	Test	Correlation	Value	p—
Female	6–Normal	70	Stanford-Binet	r	.66	<.01
Male	6–Normal	69	Stanford-Binet	r	.29	<.05
Female	9–Normal	68	Arthur Point Scale	r	.20	NS
Male	9–Normal	66	Arthur Point Scale	r	.17	NS
Female	10–Normal	67	WISC—FS	rho	.28	<.05
			WISC—Verbal	rho	.36	<.01
			WISC—Performance	rho	.34	<.01
Male	10–Normal	67	WISC—FS	rho	.19	NS
			WISC—Verbal	rho	.24	.05
			WISC—Performance	rho	.10	NS
Male	10–Normal	30	WISC—Verbal Factor	r	.38	<.05
			WISC—Attention Factor	r	.00	NS
			WISC—Performance Factor	r	.10	NS
Male	10–Normal	24	Binet Vocabulary	r	.35	.10
Female	14–Normal	26	Stanford-Binet	r	.30	.10
Male	14–Normal	20	Stanford-Binet	r	.23	NS
Female	Adolescent Emot. Disturbed	38	Wechsler-Bellevue FS	rho	.36	<.05
			Wechsler-Bellevue Verbal	rho	.29	.05
			Wechsler-Bellevue Performance	rho	.40	.01
Male	Adolescent Emot. Disturbed	52	Wechsler-Bellevue FS	rho	.07	NS
			Wechsler-Bellevue Verbal	rho	.20	.10
			Wechsler-Bellevue Performance	rho	−.04	NS
Male	Adult Normal, Superior	20	Wonderlic—Form D	rho	.00	NS
Male	Adult, Neurotic Superior IQ & Ed.	19	Wechsler-Bellevue FS	rho	−.08	NS
Male	Adult, Neurotic	25	Wechsler-Bellevue FS Factored Tests	rho	.26	NS
Female	7–Normal	18	PMA—Total IQ	rho	.35	<.10 >.05
			PMA—Motor	rho	.32	NS
			PMA—Quantitative	rho	.06	NS
			PMA—Perceptual Speed	rho	.41	.05
			PMA—Verbal	rho	.23	NS
			PMA—Spatial	rho	.22	NS
Male	7–Normal	16	PMA—Total IQ	rho	.21	NS
			PMA—Motor	rho	.47	.05
			PMA—Quantitative	rho	.11	NS
			PMA—Perceptual Speed	rho	.33	NS
			PMA—Verbal	rho	−.02	NS
			PMA—Spatial	rho	.52	<.05 >.01
Female	8–Normal	14	PMA—Total IQ	rho	.24	NS
			PMA—Motor	rho	.10	NS
			PMA—Quantitative	rho	.24	NS
			PMA—Perceptual Speed	rho	−.02	NS
			PMA—Verbal	rho	−.12	NS
			PMA—Spatial	rho	.43	<.10 >.05

TABLE XIV (Cont.)

RIRS AND INTELLIGENCE

Sex	Age and Group	N	Test	Correlation	Value	p—
Male	8–Normal	18	PMA—Total IQ	rho	.17	NS
			PMA—Motor	rho	−.03	NS
			PMA—Quantitative	rho	.28	NS
			PMA—Perceptual Speed	rho	.04	NS
			PMA—Verbal	rho	.38	<.10 >.05
			PMA—Spatial	rho	−.14	NS
Female	Adolescent Emot. Disturbed	38	Calif. Ment. Maturity-Memory	rho	.10	NS
			Calif. Ment. Maturity-Space	rho	.21	NS
			Calif. Ment. Maturity—Logic	rho	.21	NS
			Calif. Ment. Maturity-Numbers	rho	.04	NS
			Calif. Ment. Maturity-Verbal	rho	.01	NS
			Calif. Ment. Maturity-Language	rho	.18	NS
			Calif. Ment. Maturity-Non-lang.	rho	.10	NS
Male	Adolescent Emot. Disturbed	53	Calif. Ment. Maturity-Memory	rho	.10	NS
			Calif. Ment. Maturity-Space	rho	−.21	≈.14
			Calif. Ment. Maturity-Logic	rho	.03	NS
			Calif. Ment. Maturity-Numbers	rho	.05	NS
			Calif. Ment. Maturity-Verbal	rho	.11	NS
			Calif. Ment. Maturity-Language	rho	.08	NS
			Calif. Ment. Maturity-Non-lang.	rho	.17	NS

with intelligence measures at about the same level as Rorschach *M* (Levine, Spivack & Wight, 1959).

CORRELATIONS WITH ACHIEVEMENT MEASURES

Measures of scholastic achievement were available to us in four groups of children. While the correlations of intelligence and academic achievement measures are generally high, and thus intelligence might serve as the common factor in any significant relationship between RIRS and achievement measures, we still thought it worth while examining the RIRS-academic achievement relationship since the RIRS-IQ relationship is low.

We anticipated that since RIRS is a measure of a type of language richness, that RIRS scores would correlate more highly with those academic areas which emphasize language (e.g., reading) than with arithmetic. Clinical observations during Rorschach testing had also suggested to us that individuals yielding high RIRS scores frequently seemed to like to "perform" well. This gave us the impression that such individuals might be achievement oriented in attitude, and that this might be reflected in their school work.

Table XV summarizes the results. The correlation coefficients

TABLE XV

RIRS AND ACADEMIC ACHIEVEMENT

Sex	Age	N	Test	Correlation	Value	p—
Female	8–Normal	66	Reading Achievement	r	−.15	NS
			Spelling Achievement	r	−.07	NS
			Arithmetic Achievement	r	.07	NS
Male	8–Normal	66	Reading Achievement	r	.42	<.01
			Spelling Achievement	r	.32	.01
			Arithmetic Achievement	r	.17	NS
Female	Adolescent Emot. Disturbed	38	Reading Total—CAT	rho	.09	NS
			Arithmetic Total—CAT	rho	−.01	NS
			Total Test—CAT	rho	.07	NS
Male	Adolescent Emot. Disturbed	53	Reading Total—CAT	rho	.21	≈.15
			Arithmetic Total—CAT	rho	.30	.03
			Total Test—CAT	rho	.25	≈.07

of RIRS with various aspects of academic achievement vary around zero for the female groups. However, the correlations for the males, while low, are positive, and several are statistically significant.

RIRS correlates best with reading and spelling achievement in eight year old boys and with arithmetic achievement in male adolescents, but not with reading. This finding is not consistent with our expectation that RIRS might correlate more highly with academic areas involving verbalization than arithmetic. While any explanation of this discrepancy is post hoc, one might argue that reading is probably the most highly emphasized skill in the early grades, while arithmetic usually does not assume as important a place in school curriculum until later. If reading is the most important skill in the earliest grades then it is reasonable that reading as a subject area would be more likely to elicit strong achievement motivation. The correlation of reading and spelling achievement with RIRS in the eight year old boys would be consistent with our clinical impression that high RIRS individuals tend to be achievement oriented.

In the adolescent boys, RIRS correlated with arithmetic achievement test scores, but not with reading achievement. Studies of achievement test performance of emotionally disturbed adolescents at Devereux Schools have shown that California Achievement Test (CAT) arithmetic scores are frequently depressed one or more grade levels when compared with reading achievement scores. This discrepancy has been attributed to a lack of directed effort in the arithmetic section which results in careless performance. Educational psychologists at Devereux consider the arithmetic achievement score as much an indicator of effort and motive to achieve as a measure of skill with numbers. The reading subtest is not thought to require the same level of effort. If one accepts this interpretation of CAT scores, then it appears that RIRS again correlates best with the test eliciting the greatest achievement motivation. Our present post hoc interpretation would argue that achievement motivation is best elicited by reading tests in eight year olds and by arithmetic tests in older adolescents. RIRS shows the pattern of correlation with these measures that it does because it too reflects achievement motivation to some extent.

Since the data in the male groups seemed consistent with our clinically derived "hunch" that RIRS may be related to achievement motivation, we undertook to study the relationship more directly. McClelland kindly permitted us to score the Rorschach records for the 30 male Ss who had participated in the original study of n Ach (McClelland *et al.*, 1953). The n Ach scores were those obtained by McClelland's scorers from TAT. The Rorschach records were scored for RIRS without knowledge of the n Ach scores. The rank order correlation between RIRS and n Ach was $+ .36$ ($p < .05$). Male Ss who produce high RIRS scores tend also to have high n Ach scores.

We also examined the correlation between RIRS and n Ach as measured by the Edwards Personal Preference Schedule in a group of eighty-four male college students. High n Ach Ss did have a somewhat higher mean RIRS score (2.35) than low n Ach Ss (mean 2.02), but the difference was not statistically significant. McClelland (1958) has argued that measures from two projective type tests tend to correlate, but measures from projective and pre-coded, questionnaire type tests do not correlate very well. It may be that our findings reflect this same limitation. In support of such a limit we note that correlations of RIRS with intelligence measures also tend to be somewhat higher with individually administered intelligence tests which permit free responses, than with group tests.

SUMMARY OF INTELLIGENCE AND ACHIEVEMENT TEST DATA

The data reveal a low, but relatively consistent correlation of RIRS with measures of intelligence in both sexes, and a low, but relatively consistent correlation of RIRS with measures of scholastic achievement in males, but not in females. The sex differences in the relationship between RIRS and academic achievement measures are curious, and worthy of note. While the correlations of RIRS with *intelligence* measures are higher in females than in males, the opposite holds true for the relationship between RIRS and *achievement* test scores. We have no explanation for these findings. They do, on the other hand, emphasize that sex differences may not be disregarded in work with RIRS. A significant correlation of RIRS with n Ach, as measured from TAT, suggests that RIRS taps common elements with n Ach in males.

Chapter VII

DEVELOPMENTAL TRENDS

THE RORSCHACH TEST is a much used instrument for studying the psychological development of children. Ford (1946) has summarized some of the work in this area, while Wohlwill (1960) has reviewed studies of perceptual development in children, as revealed in the Rorschach test. There are a number of changes which take place in Rorschach records, with increasing maturity. Because there are age related changes in Rorschach records we felt it would be important to have developmental data. Developmental data would provide some tentative normative material, and the demonstration of a developmental change in score would also provide the basis for an interpretation of RIRS scores in developmental terms.

THE LEDWITH STUDY

We have been extremely fortunate in having had access to all of the records collected by Ledwith (1959) in her longitudinal study of Pittsburgh school children. The characteristics of Ledwith's sample and her method of selecting children are described in detail in her book. Suffice it to say that her group was a stratified random sample of public, private and parochial school children of six years of age in Pittsburgh and Allegheny County. The original sample represented approximately one child per thousand in that area. Ledwith's group is one of the most carefully chosen and followed of any group ever studied with the Rorschach test. Ledwith's sample matched 1950 census figures for Pittsburgh and environs for race, religion, and socio-economic background. The distribution of IQ scores (Stanford Binet, form L) was normal with a mean of 104 and a standard deviation of 14.0.

The children were first examined at CA six years, eight months and were examined every year up through CA eleven years, eight months. One-third to one-half of the children were followed at ages thirteen, fourteen and seventeen as well. The Rorschach test was administered with simple instructions, and minimal encouragement. Encouragement to respond further came only if the child gave one response to the first card. Thereafter there were no further comments, and inquiry was conducted after the set of ten cards had been shown to the child.

Table XVI presents the means and standard deviations of the

TABLE XVI

MEANS AND STANDARD DEVIATIONS OF RIRS SCORES
IN LEDWITH'S LONGITUDINALLY STUDIED CHILDREN

Age

	6	7	8	9	10	11	13	14	17
N	69	69	69	69	69	69	38	22	27
Male Mean	1.38	1.42	1.53	1.61	1.56	1.67	1.71	1.84	2.19
SD	.44	.54	.58	.55	.58	.65	.71	.69	.81
N	70	70	70	70	70	70	39	27	33
Female Mean	1.61	1.40	1.55	1.70	1.69	1.64	1.78	1.84	2.03
SD	.74	.65	.61	.60	.93	.81	.96	.69	1.12

distributions of RIRS scores at each level. In both boys and girls there appears to be a rather slow but steady progression toward higher and higher RIRS scores with increased age. The rank order correlation between age and RIRS means is .98 in the boys and .88 in the girls.

It is possible that the increases in scores in Ledwith's groups are a function of the sheer repetitions of the test. We do not believe this is the case. Other data indicate that repeated tests do not necessarily show increases. When the test was repeated three times in one week with a group of adults (see chapter on Reliability: Loveland and Thaler-Singer, 1959) the median RIRS barely changed at all from the first examination. However, if we could show that the scores increased with increasing age in a *cross sectional* study, the hypothesis that RIRS scores increase with age would be strongly supported.

THE GESELL INSTITUTE STUDY

Ames *et al.*, (1952; 1959) working at the Gesell Institute, have conducted such a study of children from age two to age sixteen. The Gesell Institute children represent a far different sample than Ledwith's, and the technique of administration of the test differs grossly from Ledwith's. The Gesell Institute examiners were much freer about inquiring and questioning during the course of the free association. In scoring the Gesell Institute records, we adopted a convention that material produced after a second question following a response would not be scored. The Gesell Institute records in their entirety are neither purely longitudinal in nature nor are they exclusively cross sectional. Rather, some children were newly examined at each age level, and some had already been examined at least once before. Our needs required a cross sectionally studied group, and so we selected out only those cases who had been tested for the first time at each age level. About all we can say of these children is that the chronological age of each group of Ss increases regularly. We are working with a very tenuous assumption that the groups we finally selected from the Gesell Institute samples varied only with respect to age.

Table XVII presents the means and standard deviations of the distributions of RIRS scores at each age level. Because of sampling differences and because the tests were administered under somewhat different conditions, it is not meaningful to make comparisons between the levels of the means in the Gesell Institute and Ledwith samples. It is more pertinent to see whether there is any systematic increase in the scores with increasing chronological age.

In this Gesell Institute sample, the scores apparently do tend to increase with age in the girls, albeit somewhat unsteadily, but not in the boys. The rank order correlation between means at the various age levels and chronological age is .86 in the girls. The same correlation is .21 in the boys. These figures for the girls support the hypothesis of increasing score with increasing age.*

---

* Investigation with larger samples might reveal a non-monotonic relationship between RIRS and age. The variations in scores after age twelve might reflect some real change in psychological functioning in both sexes in early adolescence.

TABLE XVII

MEANS AND STANDARD DEVIATIONS OF RIRS SCORES IN THE GESELL
INSTITUTE'S CROSS SECTIONALLY STUDIED CHILDREN

				Sex			
		Male				Female	
Age	N	Mean	SD		N	Mean	SD
2	16	.69	.33		18	.86	.65
2½	14	.71	.47		18	.67	.48
3	16	1.10	.57		16	.90	.42
3½	15	2.29	.93		17	1.05	.56
4	18	1.71	1.23		17	1.35	.66
4½	20	1.20	.59		20	1.46	.96
5	21	1.66	.59		22	1.33	.96
5½	23	1.73	1.24		22	1.30	.75
6	21	1.87	1.13		19	1.66	.91
7	22	1.95	.95		20	1.80	.74
8	22	2.02	.72		16	1.84	.58
9	21	2.41	1.25		18	1.58	.68
10	43	1.81	.68		54	1.80	.94
11	34	2.00	.74		18	1.73	.69
12	27	1.78	.63		22	1.92	.93
13	18	1.59	.60		22	1.48	.57
14	23	1.58	.64		17	1.88	.61
15	21	1.37	.59		25	1.67	.75
16	27	1.53	.73		32	2.12	1.26

In view of the sampling problem, conclusions regarding the same developmental process in boys must be held in abeyance.

NEED FOR AGE NORMS

It would appear that for girls, and probably for boys, RIRS scores increase roughly as a function of chronological age. In children, it would seem advisable to consider RIRS scores against adequate age norms, if the scores are to be useful. The means and standard deviations we have presented can serve only as the roughest norms. In the absence of a sizable sample, adequately representative of the total population, and collected with the test administered under constant instructions, it is apparent that those working with RIRS should develop age norms for their own installations.

We have suggested that RIRS may be useful in comparing records taken at different times. If there are growth related changes in children then any comparison of two or more records for the same child, taken one or more years apart, must be evaluated against developmental expectations.

INTERPRETATION OF DEVELOPMENTAL DATA

There were two purposes in evaluating developmental changes in RIRS scores. The first purpose was to provide at least a rough framework of normative material for the evaluation of RIRS scores in children. The second purpose was to provide the basis for an interpretation of RIRS in developmental terms. If it were possible to identify more "mature" and less "mature" styles of dealing with the problem posed by responding to the inkblots, perhaps any record could be interpreted in these terms.

It is not surprising that the RIRS scores appear to increase with increasing age. That the variety and quantity of language at the command of a child should increase as he grows older and is educated to use the language, is only to be expected. If anything, one might be surprised that the growth in scores was not a steeper and more regular function of age. Our data suggest that as children grow older, they tend to respond to the instructions to "tell me everything you see in the card" by describing each "thing" with more elaborate language. Other than reflecting the educational development of the children, what meaning does such an increasing use of the language have in terms of personality development?

Murphy (1947) writes that personality organization changes from the global and diffuse to the specific and the integrated, and that as far as the perception of self and others is concerned, the increasing differentiation is accompanied by, if not supported by, an increasing use of more and more specific names for parts, for people, for objects and for feelings. Osgood (1953) and Dollard and Miller (1950) have pointed out the utility increasingly varied language may have in mediating even finer and more complex discriminations, and Rogers (1951) has emphasized the role of labeling in integrating experience and sensations into the self. Luria (1961) also suggests language comes to participate in the self regulation of behavior as a function of age. It is possible then that an increasing availability, variety and quantity of language reflects increased possibilities for relating to one's self and to one's environment.

A developmental interpretation of RIRS scores would involve the dimensions of diffuseness of personality organization, and subtlety and precision in the perception of self and others. Perhaps lower scores at any given age may represent a lesser degree of complexity of personality organization. There may be a greater tendency toward simpler reactions such as withdrawal, or the "acting out" expressed in hyperactivity, hyperaggressivity, temper tantrums, poor frustration tolerance and other manifestations of "diffuse discharge of tension."

Higher scores at any given age level, indicating the availability of a greater variety and quantity of language, might be expected to go along with a greater differentiation of personality organization, as expressed in more complex layering of defenses, and a greater tendency toward more complicated reactions such as elaborate fantasy, more deliberate behavior, more specific reactions involving guilt and depression and less tendency toward the unmodulated, diffuse type of discharge of tension. However, a linear relationship between "maturity" and RIRS scores may not hold. Exceptionally high RIRS scores may sometimes be produced by individuals whose behavior reflects a caricature of rational thought and action. As indicated elsewhere, scores should be interpreted in light of other features of a test record.

At this point, it should be stated that the RIRS score probably has a number of complex determinants, and that the interpretation in developmental terms is but one way of looking at the material. The possibility that there is a developmental increase in scores has led us to consider this one dimension of interpretation in developmental terms. It should be emphasized that it is still necessary to muster specific evidence to support this interpretation. This sort of developmental interpretation may serve an heuristic function for ourselves and others who may be interested in working with RIRS.

Chapter VIII

RIRS AND QUESTIONNAIRE MEASURES OF ANXIETY AND REPRESSION

THE ANXIETY DIMENSION

Rᴇᴘʀᴇssɪᴏɴ, as a form of defense, is designed to control anxiety and we therefore expect an intimate relationship between repression and anxiety. Clinical material has suggested (see Chapter XI) that male patients with chronic anxiety give more repressed Rorschach records than controls, but it is not clear that individuals who admit to symptoms related to anxiety on questionnaires, would give more repressed Rorschach records.

Ericksen and Davids (1955) have hypothesized that "low anxiety" as measured by the Taylor Manifest Anxiety Scale (MAS) would be related to the defense of repression, while "high anxiety" Ss would be intellectualizers. Clinical interviews with twenty normal male college students provided a criterion measure of use of repression as a defense. Negative correlations of the Taylor MAS and the Pt scale of the MMPI with clinical judgments of "repression" tendencies supported Ericksen's and David's hypothesis. The MAS scale was also shown to correlate very highly with the Pt scale of the MMPI in this study.

Since in our own thinking, the high RIRS scorers should be identified with the obsessional-intellectualizing end of the personality scale, and low scorers with the repressive-hysteric end, we anticipated that RIRS scores would be positively related to Pt scores and to MAS scores. Schwartz and Kates (1957) administered Rorschachs to female college students who had been selected as representing extremes on the Taylor MAS. There were twelve high scoring Ss and twelve low scoring Ss. The mean RIRS for the high MAS group was 1.30 and for the low MAS, 1.60. This difference was not significant. It should be pointed out however, that these Rorschach records were all exceedingly "repressed" compared to other college student records we have scored.

82

For other purposes, Jerome L. Singer (personal communication) had collected Cattell's IPAT (Cattell & Scheier, 1961) and group Rorschachs from forty-nine college women and twenty-five college men. In neither group was there any significant relationship of RIRS with the covert anxiety score, the overt anxiety score or the total anxiety score of Cattell's questionnaire. However, in the males a nonsignificant r of − .21 was obtained with the overt anxiety scale.

Sarason permitted us to examine the Rorschach records of groups of boys and girls who were selected as high anxious and low anxious individuals based upon his "test anxiety" scale (Sarason *et al.*, 1960). In these groups there was no significant difference in RIRS between high and low anxiety Ss in either sex. None of the mean differences were large, but inspection of the means suggested low anxiety was associated with high RIRS scores in boys, while the opposite seemed to be true of girls. However a statistically significant anxiety scale score by sex interaction could not be demonstrated.

Because we were also interested in the correlation of RIRS with various MMPI scales, we administered the group Rorschach and the MMPI to ninety-two college males and sixty-three college females. To facilitate examination of results, we selected out all of those Ss, both males and females, who had an RIRS under 2.00. We also selected all of those males who scored 3.50 or more, and those females who scored 3.00 or more. These values were chosen arbitrarily, but they represent approximately the upper and lower quartiles of the distributions of RIRS scores for the college group. There were fifteen high RIRS females and nineteen low RIRS females. Among the males, there were twenty-four high RIRS Ss, and twenty-one low RIRS Ss. Relationships to MMPI scales were examined separately in each sex.

The mean Welsh anxiety (A) score for high RIRS males was 8.9, and for the low males, 12.0. This difference was not significant by *t* test (see Table XVIII). The A score for high RIRS females was 13.8, while the mean for the low RIRS females was 10.9. This difference also was not significant by *t* test. However, the high RIRS *males* and the high RIRS *females* are significantly different from each other. The mean difference in A score yields a *t* of 2.03

TABLE XVIII

MEAN ANXIETY SCALE SCORES IN MALE AND FEMALE
HIGH AND LOW RIRS SUBJECTS

| | | Males | | Sex | | Females | |
RIRS	N	A Score	SD		N	A Score	SD
High	24	8.9	6.1		15	13.8	7.6
Low	21	12.0	7.9		19	10.9	5.4

which is significant at $p = .05$. There is no statistically significant difference between low scoring males and females. These data reveal a significant "interaction" between sex of the S and RIRS in relation to A scores.

Although there is probably a high correlation between the MMPI Pt scales and the anxiety scale, it was still felt worthwhile examining the Pt scale separately. The mean Pt T score, corrected for K, in the high RIRS females was 56.9. In the low RIRS females, the mean was 55.3. This difference was not significant by *t* test. Among the males, the high RIRS Ss had a mean Pt score of 56.5, but the low RIRS Ss obtained a mean of 60.1. This difference is also not significant by t test. There seemed to be a trend in the data for the low RIRS males to have *higher* Pt scores and for the low RIRS females to have *lower* Pt scores than their respective high RIRS groups. A *t* test of the difference between Pt scores in low RIRS males and females was not significant, but the possible sex difference, similar in direction to what we had seen with the A scale, was intriguing enough to encourage us to examine the data further.

The current trend in MMPI interpretation is toward dealing with the profile as a whole rather than with the absolute magnitude of the scores. Following this practice, we determined the three scales which were coded high and low for each S. Among the high RIRS males, the Pt scale was coded high for but five Ss, or 21 per cent of the group (see Table XIX). Among the low RIRS males, the Pt scale was coded high for ten Ss, or 48 per cent of the group. A chi square test of this difference was significant at about the 15 per cent level of confidence ($X^2 = 2.5$; df $= 1$), indicating low RIRS males more often tended to have profiles with the Pt scale standing relatively high.

Among the females, exactly the opposite result seems to occur.

TABLE XIX

PER CENT OF HIGH AND LOW RIRS SUBJECTS
WITH PT SCALE CODED HIGH

RIRS	N	Male Per Cent	N	Female Per Cent
High	24	21%	15	53%
Low	21	48%	19	16%

Of the fifteen high RIRS females, eight, or 53 per cent had the Pt scale among their high three scales. Of the nineteen low RIRS females, only three, or 16 per cent had the Pt scale coded high. This difference yielded a chi square of 3.82, which, for one df, is significant at approximately the .05 level of confidence.

If we compare the proportion of high RIRS females who had the Pt scale coded high with the proportion of high RIRS males who had the Pt scale coded high, the chi square is significant between the .05 and .10 levels of confidence (chi square $= 2.98$; $df = 1$). If we compare the low male and female RIRS Ss for proportions with Pt scale coded high, a similar situation holds. The chi square (3.26; $df = 1$) is significant between the .05 and .10 levels of confidence. Although the results are not quite significant statistically, they suggest the presence of an interaction again. The female high RIRS Ss more often than male high RIRS Ss have the Pt scale coded high. Among the low RIRS Ss, the males more often have the Pt scale coded higher than the females.

INTERPRETATION OF FINDINGS WITH ANXIETY MEASURES

Most of the findings using the various anxiety scales are at a borderline level of statistical significance, and none of the relationships are strong. Nonetheless, the trends seem to point in the same direction. In Singer's group using the Cattell scales, the correlation in males had a negative sign. In Sarason's children, using his test anxiety scale, the relationship appeared negative in males, but positive in females. In the college group, using the A scale and the Pt scales, the relationship of RIRS to the anxiety scales is negative in sign in the males, and positive in sign with the females. Only the Schwartz and Kates sample of college women do not show the same trend. However, for a college group, the RIRS scores were exceptionally low, suggesting Ss were responding to the Rorschach test with considerable constraint in the Schwartz and Kates experiment.

If these results have meaning, they suggest that the RIRS score has different significance in the two sexes. This is a most curious finding, but we have obtained evidence of similar sex differences elsewhere (e.g., see Chapter X). These findings, tentative as they are from the statistical viewpoint, would seem to be important. Our results suggest that the functions tapped in RIRS enter into the psychological structure of males and females in different ways. The theoretical significance as far as personality organization is concerned is not yet clear. However, at the very least, the results suggest that studies using RIRS should be carried out with due consideration of sex differences in the relationship of RIRS to criterion measures.

THE REPRESSION-SENSITIZATION DIMENSION: MMPI SCALES

The repression-sensitization dimension of personality has come in for considerable study in recent years. This dimension has usually been defined in terms of scores on various of the MMPI scales. In general, items in which the subject admits to "psychopathology" are contrasted with items in which the subject denies psychopathology. Among the other measures which have been employed from the MMPI (Welsh & Dahlstrom, 1956) are Hanley's defensiveness scale, Welsh's R or repression scale, Welsh's internalization ratio, the K scale, the Hy minus Pt scales, and Byrne's (1961) repression-sensitization scale.

In seeking to examine the concurrent validity of RIRS, we undertook to examine the relationship to other measures which purport to measure the same or a similar dimension. The group Rorschach and the MMPI had been administered to ninety-two male and to sixty-three female college students. The relationships to MMPI scales were examined separately in each sex.

For the most part, the results may be summarized quickly and briefly. There were no significant differences between RIRS groups for the Repression scale, the internalization ratio, the admission scale of the Hy, the denial scale of the Hy, Hanley's defensiveness scale, the K scale, or the repression-sensitization scale. For the most part, RIRS seems to represent something which is independent of what we thought might be a similar dimension measured on the MMPI. Cattell's (1955) warning that one should not make a semantic error by identifying concepts by communalities in the verbal description of the concept, is well taken.

Another score from the MMPI which has been used to define the repression-sensitization dimension has been the difference between the Hy and the Pt scales. The distribution of differences between Hy and Pt was obtained separately for the males and females and the relationship to RIRS examined. Among the males, sixteen of twenty-four high RIRS Ss fall above the median of the Hy minus Pt distribution, while only seven of twenty-one low Ss fall above the median. This difference yields a chi square significant at the .05 level of confidence (3.91; df = 1). There is no such relationship in the female group. Once again, a relationship reveals itself in one sex, but not in the other. This one relationship may reflect the difference in Pt scale scores we have described above and from this viewpoint should not be considered an independent result.

THE AUTHORITARIAN (F) SCALE

The F scale has also been suggested as a measure of repression tendencies by Kogan (1956). Kogan argued that repression of hostile attitudes toward the parent figure is a characteristic defense of the authoritarian personality. He felt, therefore, there would be differences in recognition thresholds for stimuli consisting of disparaging aggressive and sexual references to parent and self. Kogan confirmed his hypothesis.

We administered the F scale to fifty-five emotionally disturbed male adolescents, and forty-one emotionally disturbed female adolescents, all of whom were in residence at the Devereux Schools. Rorschach records had been administered to all of these Ss as part of a regular psychological examination. These records, some of which were two years old, were rescored for RIRS. The results showed no relationship between RIRS and F scale scores in either sex.

SELF-IDEAL DISCREPANCY SCORES

Altrocchi, Parsons and Dickoff (1960) defined repressors and sensitizers by an elaborate formula from the MMPI. This group showed that repressors and sensitizers differed when examined for the *self-ideal discrepancy* determined from the Leary interpersonal checklist. The self-ideal discrepancy score may have some significance as a measure of "repression."

Young (1959) had administered the Holtzman inkblots to forty-eight college males and forty-four college females, and these records were available to us. He also administered Worchel's self-activity inventory (Worchel, 1957). Worchel's inventory provides a self-ideal discrepancy score. The self-ideal discrepancy score was studied in the high and low RIRS males and females. Low scorers were defined as those who obtained an RIRS under 2.00. There were fifteen females and twenty-one males selected as low scorers. High scorers were defined as those who fell approximately in the upper third of the distribution of RIRS scores for their sex. There were seventeen males and fifteen females selected as highs. The cut-off points were established without reference to the self-ideal discrepancy scores. Table XX presents the median

TABLE XX

MEDIAN SELF-IDEAL DISCREPANCY SCORES IN
HIGH AND LOW RIRS MALES AND FEMALES

RIRS	Male		Female	
	N	Median	N	Median
High	17	29	15	49
Low	21	53	15	38

self-ideal discrepancy scores in high and low RIRS males and females. The higher the score, the greater the discrepancy.

A U test shows the difference between high and low males is significant at approximately the .10 level of significance (U = 106.5); the difference between high and low females is significant by U test also at approximately the .10 level of confidence (U = 73.5), but the direction of the difference is exactly the opposite to that found in the males. The difference between the high RIRS males and the high RIRS females is significant at about the .15 level of confidence (U = 92.0). The difference between low RIRS males and low RIRS females is significant at the .05 level of confidence ($U = 92.0$).

Again in these data, there seems to be a sex by RIRS "interaction," but one which is of borderline statistical significance. Altrocchi *et al.* (1960) have used a self-ideal discrepancy score as a measure of the "sensitization-repression" continuum, but this may not be the only meaning of the self-ideal discrepancy. Hillson and Worchel (1957) have shown the self-ideal discrepancy score is highest in "neurotic subjects with anxiety reactions." If the self-ideal discrepancy can indeed be accepted as a measure of "tension, anxiety and maladjustment" (Rothaus and Worchel, 1960), then the results with this score seem to confirm the results obtained with questionnaire measures of anxiety. High scoring females, and low scoring males seem the most likely to "admit" to feelings of anxiety.

INTERPRETATION OF QUESTIONNAIRE MEASURES

The MMPI scales which one might reasonably expect to relate to RIRS either do not, or give equivocal or borderline findings. Those scales purporting to assess the tendency to repress, to defend, or to avoid admitting to personal problems and symptoms have little in common with RIRS. A detailed view of the various scales suggest they are complicated in makeup. As Wiggins (1962) points out, there are a number of sources of variance in MMPI scales. Until the contribution of all of the sources of variance is clarified, it is difficult to be sure what it is the questionnaires pick up. However, our data do suggest that there may be important sex differences in the response to these questionnaire measures. While of borderline significance statistically, the sex differences appeared in several different measures. This is an area which deserves further study.

In general, it would appear that the attempt to assess the concurrent validity of RIRS by means of questionnaire measures of "repression" has yielded either negative or equivocal results.

Chapter IX

RIRS AND THE INNER FRAME OF REFERENCE

R<small>APAPORT</small> (1958) has developed a theoretical view to account for the observation that man's behavior is neither totally controlled by his drives, nor is it totally controlled by conditions in his immediate environment. The fact that man has some independence of both his drives and his immediate environment is termed by Rapaport the "autonomy of the ego." "Man can interpose delay and thought not only between instinctual promptings and action, modifying and indefinitely postponing drive discharge, he can likewise modify and postpone his reaction to external stimulation" (p. 14).

Those functions which lead the organism to be oriented toward the environment and to adapt to it are those very functions which support the "autonomy of the ego from the id." One is not wholly drive ridden because the "apparatuses" of thought and perception attune man to his environment. On the other hand, it is man's drives which lead him to seek out other than what is immediately present in his environment. Thus, if the conditions which maintain reality orientation are disrupted, as in sensory deprivation, there is a decrease in the ability to pursue ordered thought, and autistic fantasies and even hallucinatory-like phenomena occur. There is then drive direction of behavior. If there is massive blocking or "repression" of drives and affects, then under these conditions Rapaport suggests the ego may well become a "slave" to environmental circumstances. The autonomy of the ego is always thought of as a relative autonomy, and presumably there are individual differences and variations in the degree of autonomy which is maintained.

SENSORY ISOLATION AND RIRS

One of the primary indications that one is in touch with drives and affects is the ability to verbalize about feeling states. The hallmark of repression is the absence of words to describe impulses and feeling states. If a repressed individual is one who is dependent upon environmental circumstances because he is out of touch with drives and feelings, then one would predict the sensory isolation situation should be more difficult for him than for one who is more in touch with inner experience. Presumably the individual more in touch with inner experience is less dependent upon outer stimulation to maintain his usual mode of functioning. He should be more receptive to inner experience. If one can conceive of the RIRS score in these terms, then the less repressed individual (the high RIRS scorer) should be more receptive and less disturbed by a situation which forces him back on inner states than the more repressed individual (low RIRS scorer).

Holt and Goldberger (1959) have studied individual differences in response to the sensory isolation situation. Sensory isolation "attenuates a person's contact with reality by cutting down the meaningful variations in sensory inputs. After a few hours, the efficiency of logical thought decreases, and there is a corresponding emergence of fantasy, dreamlike states of consciousness and vivid, hallucination-like images" (p. 1). Holt and Goldberger studied fourteen normal male college students who were exposed to eight hours of isolation. The individual was equipped so that meaningful sensory input was difficult. The subject had half ping-pong balls attached to his eyes to diffuse light. He wore heavy cotton gloves and his hands were encased in cardboard cylinders to restrict meaningful tactile sensations. The room was semi-soundproof, and the subject wore headphones which fed in white noise to minimize residual sounds from outside. The subject lay on a couch and he was instructed to report his experience verbally. These reports were transcribed. The Rorschach records were scored for RIRS without knowledge of the Ss' reactions to sensory isolation.

On the basis of the analysis of tape recordings of the subject's reaction to the situation, two syndromes of ratings emerged. The first of these was labeled "Adaptive reaction to isolation." The subject scoring high on this syndrome ". . . complies with the instruction to lie as motionless as possible and to talk freely about his thoughts and feelings, accepts and enjoys what the situation has to offer; even though he may let hypnogogic images and primary process phenomena emerge, they are under his control, for he can still think rationally when he wants to." For twelve subjects for whom complete ratings were available, the RIRS score correlated .61 (rho; $p < .05$) with the Syndrome I rating. The higher the RIRS score, the more likely the Ss were to behave in the Syndrome I manner. Holt and Goldberger rated a number of separate variables within Syndrome I. One of these had to do with the frequency and vividness of imagery and the number of senses involved in the images. The RIRS score correlated .73 (rho; $p = .01$) with the ratings of imagery. Subjects who had high RIRS scores reported more frequent and more intense sensory images. These subjects also tended to have a greater total verbal output (rho $= .51$, $p = .05$), and they tended to show more directed and logical thought (rho $= .52$, $p = .05$).

Holt and Goldberger also describe a maladaptive reaction to isolation, Syndrome II, which is orthogonal to Syndrome I. The typical subject here "spent his time dwelling on how unhappy he was, on how much he wanted to get out, and how little he was able to think connectedly; when drive directed or fantastically organized thought came into his awareness, the experience was disturbing and distorted; and at the end he made a blanket complaint when asked about his experience" (p. 25). There was no significant correlation of the RIRS scores and Syndrome II ratings (rho $= -.18$). Most of the correlations with the separate ratings going to make up Syndrome II were negative in sign, but none were significant.

Although based on a very small number of subjects, these findings suggest that the characteristics measured in the Rorschach situation carried through in the sensory isolation situation. The more an S responded to the Rorschach situation with rich and full ideation the more able he was to accept the sensory isolation situation, as predicted. Subjects who produced more "repressed" Rorschach records responded in a more constricted fashion in the sensory isolation situation.

FIELD DEPENDENCE AND RIRS

From the fact that the high RIRS Ss showed familiarity and comfortableness with their inner lives and showed less disruption of thought processes when cut off from the external frame of reference, we hypothesized that less repressed individuals are less bound by the outer, perceptual frame of reference and that they are more prone to rely on their own thoughts and images for direction. If high RIRS individuals are less repressed, they should be more in touch with their own feelings, and following Rapaport's concept, they should be less tied to environmental stimuli.

Witkin's studies of field dependence have demonstrated there are individual differences in the degree of dependence upon the external frame of reference. Witkin *et al.,* (1954) have suggested that field dependent subjects are characterized by a lack of awareness of inner life, a fear of aggressive and sexual impulses and poor control over these impulses. Field independent subjects have greater awareness of inner life and a greater effectiveness of discharge control of these impulses. Witkin's descriptions of the personality characteristics of his field dependent and field independent subjects seem in keeping with our understanding of the concept of repressive style as measured by the RIRS score and we sought to test this understanding by studying the correlation of field dependency scores with RIRS.

Witkin had rated a group of ten year old boys for their standing on a composite measure of field dependence. The final score was based upon scores in the embedded figures test, the rod and frame test, and the body adjustment series of the tilting room-tilting chair test. In this group, there was no correlation of the RIRS score with the field dependency index.

However, Witkin felt (personal communication) there may have been something atypical about this particular group, and he permitted us to examine the Rorschach records of another group of twenty-four ten year old boys for whom he also had perceptual measures. The Rorschach records were scored without knowledge of the subject's standing on the perceptual measures.

The same tests of field dependence were available for this

second group of twenty-four boys. The RIRS score correlated −.25 with the perceptual index. This correlation did not reach a statistically significant level. However, a *t* test showed a significant difference in RIRS scores, in the expected direction, between the eight most field dependent and the eight most field independent boys. While the relationship is not strong in these ten year old boys, these last results provided some small measure of support for our hypothesis. The more repressed individuals (low RIRS) showed a higher degree of field dependence.

Another opportunity to test the relationship between RIRS and field dependence was provided in data collected by Harl Young (1959). Young had administered the group form of the Holtzman inkblots to forty-eight college males and to forty-four college females. He also had administered the Rod and Frame test, the embedded figures test and Barratt's (1955) Chair-Window test to these same subjects. The Rod and Frame test and embedded figures were administered following Witkin's procedures. The Chair-Window test requires the subject to determine through which of five windows in a room one would have to look to see a chair from different angles. The Chair-Window test was found to load on a factor representing the ability to think about spatial relationships when the orientation of the body is an issue.

The RIRS scores were obtained from the group form of the Holtzman inkblots. These records were scored without knowledge of the Ss' standing on the perceptual tests. Young has shown that the three tests, Chair-Window, Rod and Frame and Embedded Figures are consistently correlated, supporting Witkin's field dependence factor. In Young's data the embedded figures test showed somewhat lower correlations with the other perceptual measures than the other measures correlated among themselves.

Table XXI presents the product moment correlations between

TABLE XXI
PRODUCT MOMENT CORRELATIONS BETWEEN MEASURES OF FIELD DEPENDENCE AND RIRS IN MALES AND FEMALES

Sex	N	RFT	EF	C-W
Males	48	−.27	−.09	.28[a]
Females	44	−.45[a]	−.19	.27

[a] Correlations of .28 or higher are significant at $p = .05$ or less.

the RIRS score and the error score on the Rod and Frame test, the mean time per item on the embedded figures test, and the number correct on the Chair-Window test.

These results provide some confirmation for the hypothesis that field dependence is associated with a low RIRS score, in both males and females. The relationship is not strong, but the magnitude and direction of the correlations are the same in the two samples.

RIRS correlates quite strongly with M responses, and M appears in the Witkin Rorschach (MFHA) formula for predicting field dependence. Young, in confirmation of Witkin, found the MHFA score did relate to measures of field dependence. Are we adding anything beyond M or the MFHA score by using RIRS? In both males and females, all correlations of RIRS with the measures of field dependence are higher than the correlations for M alone. Only one of six correlations with M alone is significant at the .05 level or better. Two of the six correlations with RIRS are significant, and two more barely miss significance at the .05 level. Where a correlation of .28 is needed for significance, the correlation coefficient proved to be .27.

Two of four correlations using the MHFA score were significant, but in every instance except one, the magnitude of correlation with RIRS is higher than with MHFA. While the amount of difference is not very large, it is nevertheless there, and at least in this instance it suggests that RIRS does add something over and beyond the contribution of the other scores.

Thomas W. Richards of the Kennedy Child Study Center has collected Rorschachs and figure drawings from 123 adult patients suffering with a variety of psychosomatic disorders (male asthma, diabetes, hypertension, dermatitis, and ulcers). He scored the figure drawings for field independence according to the criteria suggested by Witkin *et al.* (1954) and he scored the Rorschachs for RIRS. The Pearson r between two measures was .34, a value significant well below the .01 level for the number of cases.

While Richard's results provide additional evidence supporting the relationship between RIRS and field independence, it should be noted that no relationship was found between scores for figure drawings and RIRS in either males or females in Young's data.

LEVELING-SHARPENING AND RIRS

The perceptual measures and RIRS correlate in a fashion suggesting the more repressed individuals are the more field dependent. The study of response to sensory isolation suggested that the more repressed subjects were less able to function in the absence of the environmental supports to thinking. Another task pitting the inner cues (memory of stimuli) against immediate perceptual properties is the leveling-sharpening task, also called schematizing by Gardner *et al.* (1959). Two scores are derived from this task which calls for the subject to make size estimates of squares when the sizes of the squares to be judged are increasing continuously. One score represents "ranking accuracy" of the squares. "When impressions of earlier squares are not discrete, the subject has no clear scale against which to judge each new square, so that his relative estimates of the sizes of the squares tend to become inaccurate" (p. 100). A second score represents a lag in the subject's size estimates of the squares. Despite the fact that the objective stimuli increase, estimates of increasing size may lag behind the objective increase. Gardner *et al.* attribute this lag to tendencies to "assimilate" experiences to preceding ones so that distinctions between successive perceptual impressions are blurred. Gardner *et al.*, have shown that subjects who showed evidence of strong reliance on repression as a defense, as judged from the Rorschach test, also tended to be levelers. The results were confirmed in an independent sample of female university students by Holzman and Gardner (1959).

The criteria used to judge reliance on repression are described fully in Gardner *et al.* (1959). Some of the criteria, such as the absence of movement responses, stereotypy of content, vagueness, and failure to respond to one or more cards, overlap with the RIRS scoring elements. Other criteria differ, and we felt it would be of interest to determine whether RIRS related to the leveling and sharpening dimension in the same way that ratings of reliance on repression correlate with this dimension.

Holzman and Gardner had selected ten extreme levelers and

ten extreme sharpeners from a larger group of eighty female university students, ages eighteen to twenty-one. The subjects were selected on the basis of a double criterion involving both the ranking accuracy and the lag scores. The Rorschach tests had been individually administered, and were rescored for RIRS without knowledge of the Ss standing on the leveling-sharpening dimension.

First, six of the levelers had been rated by Holzman and Gardner as having a strong tendency to rely on repression as a principal defense. These six repressors had a mean RIRS of 2.26 while the other fourteen subjects had a mean of 2.62. This difference was not significant by U test, but the difference in means falls as expected. There is some degree of overlap in the rating systems.

Secondly, the mean RIRS score for levelers is 2.25 while the mean for sharpeners is 2.77. This difference is significant by U test between the five and ten per cent levels of confidence. The first five subjects in rank (low scores) for RIRS are all levelers. Gardner *et al.* (1959) report that the ranking accuracy and the lag scores correlate only to the extent of − .32. We therefore looked at the relationship of RIRS with the separate components of the leveling-sharpening dimension. RIRS correlated .16 with the lag score, but it correlated .44 with ranking accuracy. The first rank order correlation is not significant, but the second is significant at the .03 level of confidence for N = 20. RIRS seems to predict differently to the ranking accuracy and to the lag components of the leveling-sharpening score.

The significant correlation between RIRS and the ranking accuracy score suggests that the higher RIRS, the more likely that impressions of stimuli will be discrete, the discrete impressions subsequently serving as a scale or frame of reference against which new stimuli can be judged. Rich and fluid ideation serves the individual in establishing inner frames of reference which then guide and direct behavior.

INTERPRETATION OF CONSTRUCT VALIDITY DATA

What do all of these results from the study of response to sensory isolation, the study of field dependence, and the study of leveling-sharpening suggest? In each instance, results were largely consistent with our view of the construct of "repression" as measured by RIRS. In some instances the results were of borderline significance, and the correlations were never too high, but in the overall there seems to be a consistency of result which is encouraging. The results may be taken to support the view that individuals who differ on the RIRS dimension, differ with respect to availability of their own thoughts, fantasies and ideas in interpreting experience, in reliance on immediate perceptual qualities of situations, and in the tendency to establish their own frames of reference in responding to their surroundings. High RIRS Ss seem to respond to given situations by interpreting them in relation to their own ideas and their own memories. Low RIRS Ss seem to be more reliant on the immediately given perceptual qualities in a situation. They seem to look outside of themselves for the important cues. When the external frame of reference is absent, the ability of such subjects to use an internal frame of reference is limited. When the external frame of reference leads to error, as in the rod and frame task, the low RIRS S is at a handicap.

One might predict that low RIRS people would do better in situations requiring sensitivity to environmental detail. The Embedded Figures Test yields the poorest correlations with RIRS. Perhaps the reason is to be found in the fact that the Embedded Figures task also calls upon the individual's ability to be sensitive to details of the external perceptual field. If low RIRS people were more sensitive to environmental detail, one might predict that people with low RIRS scores would be better judges of the behavior of others than people with high RIRS scores. The lows would be attentive to the observable response, while the highs might be misled by personal reactions and interpretations of the behavior and predict poorly.

We are dealing with findings based upon correlations, and upon relatively low correlations to boot. However, the consistency of the correlations is encouraging in suggesting that RIRS taps a meaningful dimension of psychological functioning. One way of looking at the findings is to consider RIRS a measure of the availability of a fund of varied language, language which may be used in a mediating function to aid in coming to terms with the world. It is suggested that such a fund of language is particularly important in situations which throw an individual back upon an "inner" frame of reference. If the only frame of reference is the inner, then a fund of language may serve to orient the individual and to guide and to direct his responses. If the external frame of reference is clearer, and provides its own significance, then language may be less important as a mediator, and some more direct relationship between stimulus and response may hold. Under these circumstances it may be that individuals prone to use the inner frame of reference predominantly may have difficulty in responding appropriately to the perceptual givens.

Chapter X

SEX DIFFERENCES IN THE SIGNIFICANCE OF THE RIRS SCORE

THE TYPICAL INVESTIGATION of sex differences compares males and females for some variable, and if the means or standard deviations do not differ, the investigator is likely to conclude there are no sex differences in the particular variable. Examination of the normative data on RIRS has not shown any consistent sex difference in the means or in the distribution of the scores. However, given variables may differentiate between sexes in terms of the significance the variable has within the personality of the male and female. A score may predict a criterion variable in one sex, but not in the other, or even have opposite significance in males and females.

Such sex differences have been reported. Thus in a study of conforming behavior, Beloff (1958), Steiner (1960) and Tuddenham (1959) all report that variables which predict criteria of conformity or conventionality in men either do not predict the behavior in women, or such variables are negatively related to the criterion measure in one sex and positively related in the other sex. Sarason *et al.* (1960) have reported sex differences in the correlates of their anxiety questionnaire. Heilbrun (1961) has shown the MMPI K scale correlates positively with an independent measure of defensiveness in men and negatively in women. Rothaus and Worchel (1960) showed a significant interaction of sex with self ideal discrepancy score in the expression of hostile feelings. Where men with a *low* self ideal discrepancy reported more intense hostile feelings in relation to arbitrary frustration, women with a *large* discrepancy reported more hostile feelings under the same conditions. In studying the relationship of achievement motivation to field independence,

Honigfeld and Spigel (1960) have shown that a significant correlation of n Ach with field independence was found only in females. In males, the correlation was not significant, and in fact had a negative sign. Gardner *et al.* (1959) have found different factorial structures in males and females for tests of "styles" of cognitive and perceptual organization. Mischel and his co-workers (Personal communication) have found sex differences in the correlates of choice of delayed vs. immediate incentives. Even in as "culture-free" an area as the study of figural after-effects and apparent movement, Barthol (1958) has shown that measures of these phenomena correlate differently in males and females. Spivack and Levine (1961) found significant correlations between IQ and figural aftereffect scores in males and females but the correlation was positive in females and negative in males. The recent survey by Carlson and Carlson (1960) showing that the bulk of psychological studies are done with male Ss takes on important meaning in view of the numerous studies which show sex differences in the organization of psychological variables.

SUMMARY OF FINDINGS FROM STUDIES MENTIONED EARLIER

In studying the relationship of RIRS to various measures of "repression" and "anxiety," it was discovered that the variables sometimes correlated positively in one sex and negatively in the other, or not at all in the other sex. We shall review the various measures for which this has been true, and add some additional data in this section.

1. The relationship between RIRS and intelligence tends to be higher in females than males; the relationship between RIRS and academic achievement is higher in males than females.

2. High RIRS scoring males have a significantly lower mean Welsh Anxiety Scale score than high scoring RIRS females. There is no statistically significant difference between low scoring males and females on the Welsh A Scale.

3. Among low RIRS scoring males, there is a tendency for the Pt scale of the MMPI to be coded high more frequently than

among the high scoring males. The opposite is true for females. The high RIRS females more frequently code the Pt scale high than do the low RIRS females.

4. If one takes the Hy minus Pt distribution, then high RIRS males tend to show Hy greater than Pt, and low males the opposite. There is absolutely no relationship between Hy minus Pt and RIRS in females.

5. The discrepancy between ratings of the self and ratings of the ideal self has been used as a measure of adjustment. High RIRS males tend to have a low self-ideal discrepancy, while females with high RIRS tend to have a high self-ideal discrepancy.

SEX DIFFERENCES IN THE RECALL OF DREAMS, AND RIRS

Dreams, we believe, are means whereby impulses, wishes and unresolved feelings and conflicts receive some form of symbolic expression. If forbidden wishes are expressed through dreams, then dreams should be repressed if the recall of the dream would serve as a cue toward the arousal of the forbidden wish. From such considerations, we may hypothesize that recallers of dreams would be those least inclined toward repression, and those most inclined toward repression should recall the fewest dreams. We found some confirmation for this hypothesis in a group of schizophrenic women (see Chapter XI). In that group of women, the number of dreams reported in a given time period correlated positively and significantly with RIRS.

There was an opportunity to provide some further validation of the hypothesis in data collected by Jerome L. Singer (Personal communication). Singer had collected dreams from normal college students by asking them to keep a log of their dreams over a two week period. The Ss indicated whether they had dreamed the previous night, and how many dreams they had had. There were forty-nine complete records for women and twenty-five complete records for men. These Ss were students in a college of general studies, and were somewhat older and more experienced than the usual college class. The Ss ranged in age from twenty to fifty-two, and a number of them were married, widowed or divorced. Group Rorschachs were available, and were scored for RIRS without reference to the data on dreams.

As Table XXII shows, there is a significant positive correla-

TABLE XXII

CORRELATION OF THE NUMBER OF NIGHTS DREAMS WERE REPORTED,
AND THE NUMBER OF DREAMS REPORTED, WITH RIRS,
IN MALE AND FEMALE COLLEGE STUDENTS

	Male (N = 25)	*Female* (N = 49)
Number of nights dreams reported	−.37[b]	+.28[a]
Number of dreams reported	−.22	+.25

[a] Significant at $p = .05$.
[b] Significant at $p < .10 > .05$.

tion of the number of night dreams were reported, and RIRS in women. The women who report dreaming most frequently are those who have higher RIRS scores, those who are ideationally fluid. This finding is consistent with our view of RIRS as an index of ideational repression. However, as high a correlation, with a negative sign, is found in men. Here the men who are ideationally fluid, report dreams less frequently than the ideationally more repressed males. This finding seems at variance with our original conception of RIRS as an index of repression in males.

Singer and Schonbar (1961) have shown that dream recall frequency in women is correlated positively with Welsh's A scale, and Eichman (1961) has shown that Welsh's A scale, the Pt scale, and the Taylor Manifest Anxiety Scale all load on a common factor in women hospitalized for neuropsychiatric disorders. High RIRS in women is also associated to some degree with high Pt and high Anxiety scale scores. Also, Lachman *et al.* (1962) have shown a relationship of leveling and sharpening to frequency of dream recall in women, and RIRS is related to the leveling-sharpening dimension in women. For women the results are consistent. High RIRS is apparently related to a dimension of admission to anxiety, low repression and frequent recall of night dreams. Additional evidence of the relationship is found in the significant correlation of RIRS with the frequency of report of night dreams in schizophrenic women (see Chapter XI).

That report of night dreams should correlate negatively with

RIRS in males, is curious. Just as the high RIRS males seem to act as "repressors" on the MMPI (Hy greater than Pt), so they seem to act as "repressors" when it comes to reporting dreams. There is a consistency in these data and the data from the MMPI studies in that it is the women who follow out our conceptions of how people "should" behave, and the males who do not. Perhaps the consistency itself gives us a clue to this dimension.

Schonbar (1961) had forty-one women and four men report dreams over a period of a month. The Ss also reported the feeling tone accompanying the dreams, and judges categorized the emotional states as neutral, pleasant or unpleasant, and when unpleasant, into anxious and non-anxious. In her total sample, 108 dreams were accompanied by no or neutral affect, thirty-nine by pleasant affect, forty-three by non-anxious unpleasant and seventy-one by unpleasant, anxious feelings. Nearly half of the dreams had unpleasant affect, and of the dreams with unpleasant affect, the bulk involved anxious feelings. Since many of the dreams probably had anxious content, it is possible that the frequency of the recall of dreams depends in part upon the willingness to admit to anxious content. This kind of hypothesis would make sense. In women, high RIRS scores go along with a ready admission of anxiety, the admission to anxiety being expressed in high scores on the Pt scale and the A scale, and a frequent recall of dreams, many of which will have anxious content. Men with high RIRS scores may be much more hesitant about *admitting* to anxiety, and if the dreams of men and women are alike, then the fact that these high RIRS men report fewer dreams makes sense within this context.

SEX DIFFERENCES IN KUDER INTEREST INVENTORY

Berdie (1945; 1946) has shown that the range of interest, as measured by a recreational checklist, is related to neurosis. Normals have broader interests and they tend to be more definite in their interests than neurotics; those with a greater spread of interests also tend to have significantly more favorable MMPI profiles. Berdie worked with military populations, and with male college students.

In working with a checklist of interests, we reasoned that

more repressed Ss would have fewer differentiated interests, and would be less able to commit themselves than unrepressed Ss. Unrepressed Ss, on the other hand, should be more definite about their likes and dislikes. Their interest pattern should reveal areas of high and low interest, in contrast to the undifferentiated pattern of the repressors.

Rorschach records and Kuder Preference Records were available on a sample of twelve emotionally disturbed adolescent males and fourteen adolescent emotionally disturbed females. The Rorschach records were taken at the time of intake clinical examination, and the Kuders were taken some months later. Relatively few records were available because a large number of Kuders proved to be invalid. The V scale was outside of acceptable limits in nearly a third of the cases, and in other instances Rorschachs were not available.

Rank order correlations were obtained with each of the ten Kuder scales independently. None of the correlations in either males or females was significant statistically.

Count was made of the number of scales which stood higher than the 75 percentile or lower than the 25 percentile, and high and low RIRS Ss were compared in each sex separately. High and low RIRS was defined by the median of the distribution in each sex. Table XXIII shows the results for males and females separately.

TABLE XXIII

MEAN NUMBER OF KUDER SCALES FALLING OUTSIDE THE 75TH AND 25TH PERCENTILES IN MALE AND FEMALE ADOLESCENTS (Ns ARE GIVEN IN PARENTHESIS IN THE TABLE)

RIRS	Male	Female	U Test	p
High	7.1 (N = 6)	4.3 (N = 7)	1.5	.002
Low	4.8 (N = 6)	5.6 (N = 7)	15.5	NS
U test	4.5	13.0		
p	.01	.08		

There is a highly significant difference between high and low RIRS males, in the predicted direction, and a tendency toward difference between the high and low RIRS females in the opposite direction. High RIRS males and high RIRS females are clearly different in their response to the Kuder. The results show that high RIRS males have the most clearly delineated interests, while it is the high RIRS females who have the least clearly defined interests.

This time it is the males who are behaving according to prediction. As ideationally unrepressed individuals, the high RIRS males express very consistent likes and dislikes, and the low RIRS males have a less differentiated interest pattern. The females, on the other hand, behave in the opposite manner. The least repressed individuals have the most undifferentiated interest patterns.

An equivalent analysis of Kuder performance was also done using the data of Thomas W. Richards (Personal communication). As part of a larger study of the effects of somatic illness upon social orientation, Richards obtained Rorschach and Kuder test data on VA male patients suffering various somatic illnesses (e.g., asthma, diabetes, hypertension, etc.). The mean ages of the various groups varied from thirty-nine to forty-seven. When comparisons were made between high and low RIRS score Ss, no difference was found between degree of interest scatter. No data on females were available.

This failure to replicate the earlier findings may be due to a number of factors (e.g., age, diagnosis, etc.), and emphasizes the necessity of replicating the earlier study with a larger sample of adolescents.

SCALE CHECKING STYLES ON OSGOOD'S SEMANTIC DIFFERENTIAL

The Semantic Differential technique (Osgood, Suci and Tannenbaum, 1957) is well known as an instrument for measuring meaning. Less well known is the fact that there are relatively consistent scale checking styles which Osgood *et al.* feel are related to personality and intelligence variables. Osgood's experiments have suggested that the extreme points on the scales, the "one" and the "seven," are checked most quickly. The mid-point "four," signifying no clear-cut choice, is next in rapidity of choice, while the four intermediate points, "two," "three," "five," and "six," are checked the slowest. Characteristic use of the "one" - "four" - "seven" points is thought to reflect a form of conflict resolution in which absolute decisions are made rapidly. Use of the "two" - "three" - "five" - "six" points is thought to reflect a more cautious consideration of nuances in a decision making situation.

Our previous findings, and theoretical considerations, suggest that high RIRS Ss should fall more toward the obsessive compulsive end of the continuum. Thinking more, decisions should be made in a cautious and considered manner. Low RIRS Ss, on the other hand, should fall more toward the hysterical end of the continuum, and should react in a more impulsive fashion. In this context, a more impulsive decision might be one made rapidly in extreme terms.

A total of forty-eight Ss were used in this study (Spivack, Levine, and Brenner, 1961), selected from a pool of 141 male and female undergraduates enrolled in introductory psychology courses. The basis of selection was S's RIRS score derived from a group Rorschach administered in class. Four contrasting subgroups were formed, with twelve Ss in each group. There were high and low RIRS male groups, and high and low RIRS female groups. The equivalent groups were composed from the extreme cases on RIRS, but the groups were matched for RIRS and age.

Some months after the group Rorschach had been administered, the Ss were seen individually to partcipate in "an experiment on artistic inspiration." Each S was called in individually and asked to make ten art products, using felt forms (the procedure was something like a mosaic test). After S had completed each piece of art work, he was asked to use eleven semantic differential scales to show the meaning each piece had for him. At the end of the experiment, each S was asked to rate himself on the set of eleven semantic differential scales.

Scales were selected for use on the basis of their appropriateness in rating art products, and on the basis of their factor loadings on each of the four factors of meaning described by Osgood and his co-workers. The scales and the factors used were as follows:

Evaluative: good-bad; optimistic-pessimistic; positive-
negative
Potency: hard-soft; heavy-light; masculine-feminine
Oriented Activity: active-passive; excitable-calm; hot-cold
Stability: stable-changeable; cautious-rash

The scale points ran from 1 to 7, and the scale designations
were balanced so that sometimes *1* was the "good" end and sometimes *7*. Instructions for use of the scales were taken directly
from Osgood *et al.* and modified only to make them meaningful
in the present situation.

Table XXIV presents the mean per cent use of the *1-7-4*, and
2-3-5-6 pattern in the four groups for the self ratings.

TABLE XXIV

MEAN PER CENT USE OF SCALE CHECKING STYLES IN HIGH AND
LOW RIRS MALES AND FEMALES, FOR RATINGS OF
SELF, AND RATINGS OF ART

	Groups							
	Low RIRS Female		High RIRS Female		Low RIRS Male		High RIRS Male	
Styles	Self	Art	Self	Art	Self	Art	Self	Art
1-7	16.7	20.4	33.1	31.8	15.9	21.2	12.9	16.9
4	22.1	21.4	23.1	26.3	24.2	21.8	14.4	15.0
2-3-5-6	61.2	58.2	43.8	41.9	59.9	57.0	72.7	68.1
Σ 1-4-7 minus Σ 2-3-5-6	−22.4	−15.4	+12.4	+16.2	−19.8	−14.0	−45.4	−36.2

Following Osgood's rationale, a score was defined for each
S employing the simple formula:Σ 1-4-7 minus Σ 2-3-5-6. This
score would then be taken as a measure of the extent to which
conflict resolution follows a pattern of rapid and/or black and
white decision making.

The Kruskal-Wallis H test of the scores for self ratings revealed significant differences among the four groups ($H = 11.9$;
$df = 3$; $p < .01$). While both the male and female *low* RIRS
groups gave comparable scores, the high RIRS *females* made
relatively extensive use of the 1-4-7 pattern, while the *high* RIRS
males made extensive use of the 2-3-5-6 pattern. In other words,
the female group, characterized by fluid, rich and unrepressed
ideation tended toward rapid, black-white decision making,
while ideationally free males revealed more cautious and carefully considered responses.

The Ss had also rated their art products. Differences in style scores for ratings of the art products were tested by means of the Kruskal-Wallace H test. Again there were statistically significant ($H = 7.9$; $df = 3$; $p < .05$) differences among the groups, closely mirroring the pattern described above for the self ratings. The fact that the same pattern of RIRS by sex interaction obtained for ratings of the self and ratings of external objects would lend support to the notion that a general stylistic feature is involved here.

As a further check upon the question of consistency in style, rank order correlations were obtained for each of the four groups between the self and non-self style scores. For the low and high RIRS females the rho's were .41, and .60; for the low and high RIRS males, the rho's were .11 and .55 (A rho of .51 is significant at $p = .05$). These coefficients suggest only modest reliability for the scale checking style. Considering the limited reliability of the checking style, the fact that the same pattern of relationship between RIRS and sex emerges lends added weight to the idea that the relationship has substance.

Osgood *et al.* (1957) have suggested that the 1-4-7 checking style may be associated with lower intelligence. We have found a modest correlation between intelligence test scores and RIRS scores, the correlation coefficients averaging around .20 for a large number of separate tests (see Chapter VI). Although it is likely that high and low RIRS Ss differ for intelligence to some degree, it is exceedingly unlikely that *male* and *female* high RIRS Ss differ for intelligence. Our results certainly cannot be attributed simply to differences in intelligence.

Since the pairs of high and low RIRS groups had equivalent total RIRS scores, and the high male and female groups behaved differently in scale checking style, the possibility arose that equivalent *total* RIRS scores might mask significant differences in the components making up the total RIRS score. The four major components of the total score are movement, specificity of the response content, elaborations upon the response content, and the specific impulse references. The four major groups were compared for the relative distributions of these four major RIRS components. Although differences appeared between high and low RIRS groups, there were no significant differences between sexes and within RIRS groups. This finding shows that high RIRS males and females, and low RIRS males and females arrive at their high or low RIRS scores in an equivalent fashion. Although both total amount of ideation and quality of the ideation are the same, the behavioral correlates in males and females are disparate.

In this instance, as with the data from the Kuder, predictions made from a consideration of the properties of RIRS are borne out in males, but the females behave in an opposite manner. Considering that high RIRS scores go along with obsessive-compulsive characteristics, the males are more cautious and considered in the choices they make. The females who are unrepressed, as indicated by high RIRS, respond more quickly, choosing the extreme ratings more frequently than the high males.

INTERPRETATION OF STUDIES OF SEX DIFFERENCES

The studies of sex differences in the correlates of RIRS are consistent in pointing to an interaction of sex and RIRS. Clearly, no single interpretive dimension is sufficient to explain the variations in patterns of intercorrelations between the sexes. While it has been useful to think of RIRS as measuring a dimension of intellectualization-repression, the data clearly suggest the limitation of such a view. While at times both males and females do function in a fashion consistent with such a dimension, at other times, the findings turn out exactly the opposite of predictions.

A simple hypothesis of one underlying dimension is obviously inadequate to account for the findings. It may be more useful to attempt to formulate a descriptive picture of males and females high and low on RIRS as this description emerges from a consideration of the available correlations. In general, the most clear-cut sex differences in the correlates of RIRS are observed in the comparison of the high males and the high females. The high RIRS female seems to admit to personal problems, worries and concerns. She reveals a large discrepancy between her view of an ideal self and her conscious self image. She readily reports dreams, many of which probably have anxious content. Her interests are not well defined, and in a decision making situation she is prone to form rapid, extreme opinions.

In contrast, the high RIRS male appears to have few personal worries and concerns. His image of an ideal self is more congruent with his image of himself. He apparently dreams less, or at least recalls fewer dreams, and this may relate to the fact that dreams frequently have anxious components. His current interests seem rather well defined, and his opinions or judgments tend to be deliberate.

One might approach these differences in males and females from at least two different vantage points. Although males and females who get high RIRS scores get them in the same way, there still may be an essential difference in the operation of language in any problem solving situation. For high RIRS females, a thought or "inner language" might serve as a cue or rationale for action; for the male, a thought may serve as a cue for another thought and therefore the delay of action. In the female, verbalization to self and others may serve an almost exclusively expressive function, while in the male, verbalization to self and others may serve much more to provide cues for a subsequent decision as to the best mode of action. This kind of view would lead to the specific hypothesis that the ties between language and action are much closer in women with high RIRS than in men. Women with high RIRS when asked to define action words (e.g., rattle, climb, move) may be much more prone to use gestures than men with high RIRS. The specific hypothesis is stated simply to indicate a possibility for testing this view. The point is simply this: If one were to adopt the view that our results show essential differences in the operation of language in male and female, one would direct attention toward language and its use in various situations.

A second viewpoint would argue that verbalized thought in men and women follows the same rules of operation, but that in decision making situations other sex-linked factors come into play in interaction with verbalized thought, leading to different behavior. Cultural roles and expectations may encompass many possible factors. It may be easier for a woman with conscious anxious thoughts to express them or "admit" to them than is the case for a male. In fact, in order not to "admit" to anxious thoughts, the male might draw upon properties of thought so as to rationalize or diminish the significance of anxious thoughts relative to his self-image. Expressing anxious thoughts, and seeking help, are more consistent with the dependent and passive elements of the female role.

High RIRS scores in both males and females may reflect the availability to consciousness of verbalizable imagery, feelings and memories with direction-giving potential for behavior. However the demand for conceptual consistency and "reasonableness" may be differential in males and females in our culture. In males, verbalized thoughts, once appearing, may more frequently be screened or categorized so as to result in consistent choices than is the case for females. In females, the relative absence of this "cultural" demand may allow for more direct manifestation of verbalized thought in action, giving behavior less consistency over time, result in more "change of mind" and lower latency of response.

The implication of the above is that if situations were structured so as to eliminate the sex-role differentiation, that the correlates of RIRS in males and females would be the same. One might predict, for instance, that high RIRS career women who have worked in a "man's" world for some years and thereby confronted the same pressures for rational decisions, would perform the same as high RIRS men when confronted with decision making situations.

The present data also have direct bearing upon diagnostic testing and clinical practice generally. No validity study can be considered complete until it has been accomplished separately in men and women. Studies which combine samples of men and women run the serious risk of missing significant findings. Correlational studies and studies which predict behavior must take the sex difference into account. Sampling theory tells us this is true, but frequently we act as if we do not believe in sampling theory.

For example, all of the cases of hysterics which we found in Rorschach textbooks were women, and all of the cases of obsessive compulsives we found in the same textbooks were men. It may be true that women develop hysterical neuroses more often than men do, and it may be true that men develop obsessive compulsive neuroses more often than women do, but both conditions are diagnosed in both sexes. Seventeen of Rapaport, Gill and Schafer's (1946) twenty hysterical neuroses were women, and nine of seventeen obsessive compulsive neuroses were women. Yet all comparisons are made for diagnostic groupings and none of the comparisons were checked by sex. About half of Rapaport *et al.*'s cases in the remaining diagnostic categories were female, but all of his controls were males. It is inconceivable that the results were not influenced by sex differences in some respects, and it is not unlikely that a whole generation of clinicians, influenced by this classic work in diagnostic testing, came away with the implicit conception that sex did not make any difference in diagnostic work.

If the data presented do nothing else for Rorschach work than to emphasize the point that the sexes must be studied separately, these findings would seem worthwhile.

Chapter XI

CLINICAL VALIDITY AND UTILITY

VALIDATION OF MEASURES of personality is typically difficult since adequate criteria of personality functioning are hard to come by. In examining the clinical utility of RIRS, we have been guided primarily by our own direct clinical experience with the measure. This experience has been sufficiently convincing to motivate us to seek to "externalize" our subjective convictions by studying RIRS within a normative frame of reference in clinical populations, and in different clinical situations.

RIRS SCORES OF "TEXTBOOK" HYSTERIC AND OBSESSIVE-COMPULSIVE CASES

From a clinical viewpoint, the typical patient who relies on repression as a defense is diagnosed as an hysteric, and the typical patient using intellectualization as a defense is an obsessive compulsive. Textbook cases of pure hysterics or pure obsessive compulsives are rarely found, but if our index is a measure of repressive tendencies, hysterics should exhibit more repression, that is have lower RIRS scores, than obsessive compulsive neurotics. The best place to look for a textbook case is in a textbook, and so our first attempt at validation involved a comparison of cases presented in textbooks as illustrative of each of these syndromes. Examinations of several well known textbooks turned up sixteen complete protocols, eight of each syndrome. The Rorschach protocols came from the original *Psychodiagnostics*, (Rorschach 1942), from Schafer (1948; 1954), from Beck (1945) and from Bochner and Halpern (1942).

The scores for the hysterics range from 1.26 to 2.90, with a mean of 1.97. The range of scores for the obsessive compulsive cases is 2.04 to 5.15, with a mean of 3.55. This difference is significant by U test at $p = .001$. The overlap in scores is rather minimal. The two hysterical cases with the highest scores (least repressed) were those described as individuals who were tested at a point at which repressive defenses and neurotic symptoms were becoming inadequate to control anxiety. Repression was not working well in these cases.

There are several problems with this sort of validation, and it should not by any means be considered anything other than "interesting and suggestive." First, the textbook hysterics are without exception women, while the textbook obsessive compulsives are without exception males. Second, there are likely to be large differences in education and intelligence between the groups since the compulsives contain several professionally trained men, and there are no equivalently trained hysterical women in the textbooks. Third, although each of the textbooks contributed almost the same number of compulsive and hysterical cases, the basis for the authors' selection of cases is not clear.

We indicated earlier that one of the ongoing problems in Rorschach work is to objectify and to quantify the insights of clinical workers. Can we quantitatively duplicate clinical judgment? Schafer (1954) presents a series of four cases, all female, as illustrations of the breakdown in the effectiveness of repressive defenses. The first case is described as a well defended individual showing "neurotic hysterical-repressive trends." The index for this case is 1.47. The second case was diagnosed as hysteric with phobic and depressive features, and is described by Schafer as showing a more precarious defensive position, but without evidence of defensive collapse. The index in this case is a little bit higher, 1.59. In the third case, the defenses and neurotic symptoms appear to be failing badly, and the index reflects this as it jumps to 2.66. In the fourth case, there is a picture of long standing multiple phobias in a patient considered a borderline psychotic. Schafer comments that the record reflects a "heavy reliance on repressive defense," and in contrast to the previous patient in the series, the index drops back to 1.92. The numerical values of the index then correlate very nicely with Schafer's judgment concerning the relative ordering of the four cases.

RIRS SCORES IN A GROUP OF NEUROTIC
AND NORMAL MALES

Repression is the hallmark of neurosis, and the function of psychotherapy presumably is to "undo" repressions. From this theoretical view one can deduce that neurotics will, in general, show the effects of chronic repression, and that normals will be relatively unrepressed. This should be particularly true when the normals are well functioning, apparently creative individuals.

As part of an in-service counseling program in an industrial firm, twenty junior executives were examined. These men were referred for counseling and evaluation by their superiors because they were considered "comers." Management was interested in these men as potential future executives. The men ranged in age from twenty-five to forty-four, and had a variety of jobs ranging from an electronic technician to lawyer and advertising art department director. Educational level ranged from 10th grade to one man who had a law degree. All but four of the men had had some college training, and the median educational level was at the bachelors degree. All but two of the men were married, and fifteen of the twenty men had been in the armed forces.

Nineteen patients were obtained from a Veterans Administration Mental Hygiene Clinic. These patients were seen for routine psychological examination. They were selected for the study either because of superior intelligence or superior education, but without reference to their Rorschach records. The patients were selected from among those with psychoneurotic diagnoses. About half of the men had diagnoses of "anxiety reaction," and the remainder one of the diagnoses indicating somatic complaints. The age range was twenty-two to forty-eight, and their positions ranged from a clerk and railroad worker to a physicist and teacher. Several of the men were self employed. Education ranged from 10th grade through the Ph.D. All but four men had some college training and the median educational level was at the bachelors degree. Full scale Wechsler Bellevue IQs ranged from 99 to 144 with a median of 120. In many important respects, the two groups seemed to be very closely equated, differing primarily in the fact that one group was under treatment for psychoneurotic difficulties, and the other was not.

The RIRS scores for the normals ranged from 1.62 to 5.29. The median RIRS was 3.28.* The scores for the psychoneurotic patients ranged from 1.58 to 7.00, the median RIRS being 2.56. The value of the U test was 119, significant at $p = .05$, two tail test. The hypothesis that RIRS would differentiate the two groups is supported.

The value of these results lies more in the demonstration that the technique differentiates groups in a way which is consistent with theory than in the precise degree of differentiation of the groups. Given the assumptions that chronic psychoneuroses are indeed based upon more or less widespread and severe "repressions," and that "repression" or chronic anxiety would be manifested in the Rorschach test through ideational impoverishment, then the results support the validity of the RIRS technique. Hopefully, if psychotherapy is directed toward lifting repression and such therapy is successful, the RIRS score should increase substantially.

Our results would suggest that chronic neurosis is related to lower RIRS scores and "normalcy" or health, in general, is related to higher RIRS scores. We must stress the phrase "in general" because there are obviously very "sick" records which produce high scores. These records must be differentiated from healthy, unrepressed records by means other than RIRS. In either event, RIRS does provide a quantitative index to the degree of ideational impoverishment, or ideational richness, and it should be of help in appreciating the patient's psychological structure.

RIRS SCORES IN PSYCHOSOMATIC PATIENTS

Clinical theory and observation suggests that psychosomatic involvement is high in patients who are more "repressed." The somatic complaints are thought to represent conflicts and feelings which are expressed through a body language rather than through other channels of expression. Frequently psychotherapy is di-

---

* R. G. Ballard points out that the median value found for obsessive compulsive neurotics is greater than that found for our normals. He argues this is evidence that the formulation concerning repression and neurosis may be overgeneralized. We agree that RIRS will *not* differentiate normals from neurotics with no overlap at all. It may be that some conditions, such as obsessive compulsive neurosis, may lead to much higher than "normal" scores.

rected toward helping such patients to apply the "proper" verbal labels for the affects experienced in various situations. From this viewpoint it might be argued that patients who have a strong somatic orientation will be more repressed than patients who seek therapy primarily for intrapsychic problems.

Sixteen of the nineteen case files of the psychoneurotic VA clinic patients had adequate data for study. Independently of knowledge of the Rorschach records, two clinical psychology trainees (under the supervision of R. G. Ballard, VA Mental Hygiene Clinic, Philadelphia) rated the records for the degree of somatic versus psychological orientation shown by the patients. The trainees agreed quite well in the ratings, disagreeing by more than one scale point (on a five point scale) in only one of the sixteen cases. Of the sixteen cases, six were rated as having predominant somatic orientation, four as having equal somatic and intrapsychic problems, and six as having predominantly intrapsychic problems. The averaged rating of somatic-psychological orientation correlated .44 (rho) with RIRS. This correlation is significant at the .05 level of confidence.

As a follow up to this study, Mary McCaulley, an interne under the supervision of Ballard, had therapists rate their case load for the degree of somatic orientation shown by their patients. From these ratings, McCaulley selected twenty-five who were high in somatic orientation and twenty-five who were low in somatic orientation. The two groups were compared for RIRS. The mean of the somatically oriented group was 1.96, while the mean of the less somatically oriented group was 2.20. This difference was not significant statistically, however.

In the total group of fifty patients, eighteen had been diagnosed as psychotic. When these were removed from the sample, the mean RIRS score for seventeen somatically oriented patients was 1.98, while the mean for fifteen nonsomatically oriented patients was 2.40. This difference yielded a t of 1.50, which is significant at about the .08 level for a one tailed test.

The two studies provide some support for each other in that they suggest that neurotic patients who are concentrated on somatic complaints will produce more repressed records than patients who have other psychological complaints. Obviously these results are no more than suggestive, and certainly the results of the second study must be considered in light of the removal of the psychotic patients from the sample.

Thomas W. Richards, of the Kennedy Child Study Center, has collected individual Rorschach records on a series of 123 male adults who were treated for psychosomatic disorders in two Veterans Administration clinics. The Rorschachs were scored by Richards using our manual. The results of this study are presented in Table XXV.

TABLE XXV

RIRS Scores for Patients Suffering with Psychosomatic Disorders and From Diabetes

Psychosomatic Disorder	N	Mean Age	Mean RIRS	SD
Diabetes	21	45.8	1.87	1.03
Asthma	20	42.0	1.41	.84
Hypertension	19	45.1	1.43	.62
Skin	20	39.5	1.42	.84
Ulcer	21	42.0	1.73	1.00
Mixed Disorders	22	47.1	1.50	.70
Total Group	123	43.7	1.56	.85

A normal control was not available to Richards. However, Richards compared the mean score obtained by Loveland and Singer's (1959) (see chapter on reliability, and appendix) army men with the total group of medical patients. Richards reported a mean of 1.87 for this normal group. When compared with the total group of medical patients by t test, the normals proved significantly less repressed ($t = 2.1$; $p = .04$, two tail test). It is also instructive to note that McCaulley's non-somatically oriented non-psychotic patients obtained a mean of 2.40, a value which is a full SD beyond the mean for Richards' total group, including the diabetics.

A comparison of the scores among the various psychosomatic groups shows that the diabetics have scores that are less repressed than the values for most of the other psychosomatic groups, although none of the differences reach an acceptable level of statistical significance. The group of diabetics differed from the group of hypertensives at approximately the .10 level of confidence, and they differed from both the asthma and skin disorders at about the .12 level of confidence. (The p values are all two tailed, and result from t tests.)

Richards' findings seem to add additional support to the hypothesis that patients with psychosomatic disorders will produce more repressed Rorschach records. The general trend of his findings is certainly consistent with those we have reported above.

RIRS SCORES IN DELINQUENTS

Delinquency in adolescents may be based upon a variety of underlying psychological problems. Character problems, neurosis, and psychosis have been diagnosed in individual cases. From the viewpoint of clinical theory, these cases all have in common the element of "acting out." Theory would suggest that "acting out" is the opposite side of the coin from neurotic fantasy, and "acting out" may be based upon heightened repression. If so, one might anticipate that "acting out," delinquent adolescents would be more ideationally "repressed" than more neurotic adolescents.

Elsewhere (Herskovitz, Levine, and Spivack, 1959), we have reported a clinical study of anti-social behavior in adolescents from upper income groups. The fifty-five adolescents were all in residence at a treatment center, and those included as members of the anti-social group had all had some degree of contact with the police or juvenile authorities because of acting out in the community. A control group of fifty adolescents referred for residential treatment, matched in age and intelligence to the "delinquents," was employed. The control group had a variety of presenting problems including poor school work, conflicts with parents at home, aggressivity or withdrawal with peers, and anxiety and somatic complaints.

The control group is probably not the most adequate for this type of study since manifestations of acting out in other than anti-social directions occurred in these cases. The major difference is that the acting out, when it did occur, was usually confined to the home situation, or was not sufficiently severe or provocative to bring the child to the attention of juvenile authorities.

Rorschach records were available for twenty-eight of the fifty-five delinquent adolescents, and for forty of the control group. The mean RIRS for the twenty-eight anti-social adolescents was 2.17 (SD = .94), while the mean for the forty control Ss was 2.34 (SD = 1.11). The *t* test was not significant. We noted that several of the boys with very high RIRS scores in the police contact group were those who had committed some form of sex offense.

The mean for five boys who had committed sex offenses (exhibitionism, attempted rape, homosexual seduction) was 3.01, all but one of the cases falling above the mean of the anti-social group. Suggestively, the "sex offenders" represent a different breed, psychologically, from those who commit other delinquencies.

The results do not confirm the hypothesis that anti-social acting out is related to greater reliance on repression. However, detailed examination of the results do suggest a similar study should be carried out, but making use of controls who themselves are less prone to "act out." Also detailed examination of the results led to the hypothesis that in contrast to other types of delinquents, adolescent males who become involved in sex offenses are less repressed. This hypothesis requires further test with much larger samples.

RIRS SCORES IN SCHIZOPHRENICS

Many years ago, Piotrowski (1938) studied a large group of schizophrenic patients who had been treated by insulin coma. Pre-treatment records, post-treatment records, and judgments of improvement or non-improvement were available on these patients. The patients were both male and female, and ranged in age from fifteen to forty-four. We had the opportunity to study seventeen pairs of the records Piotrowski used in his original study.

These schizophrenic patients yield extremely repressed records, both before and after insulin therapy. The median RIRS pre-therapy was 1.20 and the median post-therapy RIRS was 1.18. In general, these scores are low and suggest that schizophrenic records may be highly repressed.

There were unambiguous ratings of "improvement" in nine of the seventeen cases, and ratings of "no improvement" in six other cases. The improvement was not clear in two of the cases. The RIRS score did not "predict" improvement, and there was no systematic change in the improved, or in the unimproved group. However, the relative amount of change seemed greater in the improved group than in the unimproved group, if change in RIRS is taken independently of the direction of change. The six unimproved cases had RIRS changes (difference between pre and post test) ranging from .09 to .35, the median change being .20. The nine improved cases had changes ranging from .05 to 1.80, with a median of .44, this difference being significant by U test at approximately the .10 level, two tail test. It would appear then that those schizophrenics who were judged as improved, that is those whose behavior changed, also tended to change to a greater extent in RIRS, although the direction of change is apparently not systematic.

In view of the behavioral change and in view of the average retest interval of six months, the rank order correlation between the two testings of .60 is impressive. This value is significant at $p = .01$, and confirms much of the other data we have which shows substantial stability for the RIRS score.

FEMALE SCHIZOPHRENICS

The Schizophrenia Research Project at the Eastern Pennsylvania Psychiatric Institute, Philadelphia, organized by Ivan Boszormenyi-Nagy, works with young, adult, female schizophrenics. These patients were on the service because of their interest to the research group who work with various psychotherapeutic techniques. Rorschach records were available on thirty-four such women who were hospitalized and under therapy for schizophrenia. The group ranged in age from sixteen to twenty-nine, with a median of twenty-two. The educational level ranged from fourth grade to college graduates, with two thirds of the subjects having completed high school, at least. Seven of the patients had had some college. Intelligence was estimated from the vocabulary test of the 1916 Stanford Binet. Estimated IQs ranged from 67 to 140+, the median being 106. Ten of the women were Negro, and the remainder white.

RIRS scores in this group ranged from .44 to 4.87, with a median of 1.59. These scores are in general somewhat higher than the scores for Piotrowski's sample, but they seem fairly low for a population which is this well educated. However, there is no adequate control population available for this sample, and so it is difficult to say whether or not these scores are low. Our tentative conclusion is that RIRS scores may be low in schizophrenic groups, but there are most certainly subvarieties of schizophrenics who produce richer records.

There were ten Negro patients among the group of thirty-four. The median RIRS for these Negro patients is 1.14 in contrast to a median value of 1.89 for the white patients. This difference between the two groups is significant at about the .07 level of confidence by the median chi square ($X^2 = 3.54$; df = 1), and it suggests Rorschach responses may be influenced by racial considerations, or perhaps by the difference in race between examiner and patient.

There is a substantial correlation between the IQ estimate from the vocabulary test and RIRS. In a group of twenty-four white Ss, the rho is .58, significant well below the .01 level. Among the ten Negro Ss, the correlation is .62, a value which is significant below the .05 level of confidence. Both of these correlations are substantially higher than values found for females generally. These results suggest that intelligence measurement in schizophrenics is very closely related to verbal responsiveness as measured by RIRS, perhaps much more so than in non-psychotic populations. James L. Framo, who provided these data, suggested the more repressed patients were also more guarded, producing less scoreable material on the vocabulary test and on the Rorschach.

The EPPI project had ward behavior ratings, along a dimension of active-passive, made by ward personnel. A patient was classified as active or passive in terms of her social impact on ward personnel. If personnel were forced by the patient to control her, or to dampen her activities, she was rated *active*. If personnel were drawn into helping the patient, or drawing her out, she was rated *passive*. Framo, who obtained the records and the ratings, writes: "Ratings were obtained every two months for one year. There tended to be considerable stability in this dimension; that is, most of the patients maintained their active or passive positions during the year. A few, however, did change from one extreme to the other. The ratings are for the particular period in which the Rorschach was given" (personal communication).

Behavior ratings of active or passive were available for twenty-two of the thirty-four patients. The remainder were not on the ward when the ratings were collected. There were thirteen patients rated active, and nine rated passive. The median RIRS for the active patients was 1.77, while the median for the passive patients was 1.11. This difference yields a U of 28.5, which is significant at $p = .05$, two tail test. The more unrepressed patients were the more active patients. There were four Negros among the passive patients, and three Negros among the active patients. However, even if the RIRS scores for the Negro patients are removed from the sample, the medians for the two groups are unchanged.

Framo (Framo, Osterweil and Boszormenyi-Nagy, 1962)* also interviewed the patients and obtained dreams from them once every two months during the course of the year. One or more dreams was obtained from twenty-one of the thirty-four patients. The other patients were not on the ward at the time the dreams were being collected. The number of dreams collected ranged from one to eighteen, with a median of five. The correlation (rho) between the RIRS and the number of dreams reported by the patients was .36. This value is significant at about $p = .05$ for the 21 cases. This correlation is particularly interesting in view of the positive correlation between frequency of dream recall and RIRS in normal women (see Chapter X).

Data on length of hospitalization were available on thirty-two of the thirty-four patients. Two had been transferred to other institutions and an adequate estimate of the total length of their hospitalization could not be made. The median hospitalization length to discharge was nine months in the total group. The median RIRS of the sixteen hospitalized ten months or more was 1.26. The median of those hospitalized nine months or less was 1.87. This difference is not statistically significant, by U test. However, Framo comments: "One should be cautious in using hospital discharge, as a criterion alone, of improvement or 'cure.' In this research unit there is intensive individual, group and family therapy given patients. Some of the patients still hospitalized in the unit (those with the longer times to discharge) may have a potentially better prognosis than those earlier discharged, inasmuch as some seem to be undergoing basic personality changes."

Three of the patients with the longest hospitalization also had

---

* Framo *et al.* report data on ninety-two patients. The data we report here are based on the number of cases available when Framo permitted us to work with his material.

the highest RIRS scores and these three were patients who were continued in the intensive treatment program of the unit. If we exclude these three patients from consideration, the median of the group with the longest hospitalization drops to 1.17 and the difference between groups is significant statistically, by U test at $p = .02$ (U $= 50$), two tail test. In another setting, it may be that length of hospitalization can be predicted from the RIRS score. This is a problem certainly worth investigating. Perhaps female patients who are more responsive ideationally are more responsive psychologically than patients who are more constricted from an ideational viewpoint. Perhaps RIRS scores will differentiate the so-called process from reactive schizophrenics.

In this population of schizophrenic women, the RIRS seems to be relatively low, as in Piotrowski's sample of schizophrenics. In this group RIRS correlates significantly with several other dimensions of behavior. First, there is a substantial correlation with a vocabulary based IQ. Secondly, the more active patients were those with higher RIRS scores. Thirdly, patients with higher RIRS scores reported more dreams than patients with lower RIRS. All of these relationships were statistically significant. Also, there was a suggestive relationship between RIRS and length of hospitalization. Patients who produced the least repressed records tended to be hospitalized for the shortest length of time. These results suggest RIRS is related to a number of important dimensions of behavior. In particular, the higher RIRS scores may reflect greater psychological responsiveness and intactness in schizophrenic women.

RETEST RESULTS IN INDIVIDUAL CASE STUDIES

One of the major problems facing the psychologist is the use of his techniques in evaluating changes in psychotherapy. Psychotherapies are directed toward different ends in different individuals, and the results are often difficult to express quantitatively. In particular, when dealing with the single case, it is very difficult to say whether a shift in test scores is truly meaningful.

While RIRS is a mean score, a score is derived for each response in the record. One may derive a mean as a measure of central tendency in the record, and also describe the distribution of RIRS scores for the total number of responses in that record. If we treat two records for one individual as two samples taken from the universe of his responses, we can ask the question whether the records are different statistically, and we can assign a probability value to the change which occurs within a single individual, tested twice. Using RIRS, it is possible to say whether a record taken at one time is significantly different from a record taken at another time, for a single individual.

PSYCHOTHERAPIES

Psychoanalysis is specifically directed toward undoing repressions, and if psychoanalytic treatment is successful, RIRS should shift in a direction indicating lessened repression. The scores should increase. In the original *Psychodiagnostics*, Rorschach presents a case of a compulsion neurosis, treated psychoanalytically for five months. The initial RIRS score in this case was 2.04, and following therapy it increased to 2.41. By virtue of the small standard error of the difference provided by the seventy responses of each record, a t test showed the difference to be significant at the .04 level of confidence, one tail test. The decrease in repression indicated by these results is quite consonant with Rorschach's own evaluation of the change in the record.

Beck (1945) presents the pre and post analysis records of "a nationally known psychiatrist." The analysand was described clinically as having become ideationally more free and spontaneous as a result of the analysis. The pre-analysis RIRS was 3.43, while the post-therapy score was 6.12. The t test ($t = 3.90$) showed the change was highly significant statistically ($p < .001$). In both of these cases of psychoanalysis, the post-test records showed a reduction in the level of repression, as indicated by statistically significant increase in RIRS.

Psychotherapies other than psychoanalysis also result in the lifting of repression. One of us treated an adolescent for two and one-half years, with excellent results. The therapy notes reveal a remarkable change in his willingness to introspect and communicate fantasies and associations during the course of treatment, and behaviorally, there was considerable reduction in acting out. Prior to therapy, RIRS was 2.57. After two and one-half years of therapy, the index increased to 5.54. This difference between the two records was significant at $p = .02$ by U test.

Another set of records was provided by a teen age girl who had been treated in psychotherapy for about a year and a half. The pre-therapy RIRS was .75, while the post-therapy record was 1.73. This difference was significant at below the .01 level of confidence by U test. There was some improvement in this girl, in the direction of less bizarre acting out (the patient was not considered schizophrenic, however) at the point the second record was taken. This pair of records had been analyzed blindly by a well known Rorschach expert who asserted the second record revealed a somewhat more spontaneous individual. The quantitative scores paralleled his judgment very nicely in this case.

A schizophrenic adolescent girl was in residential therapy for eighteen months with a psychoanalyst who practiced a variety of Rosen's "direct analysis." The pre-therapy record showed an RIRS of 2.50, while the record eighteen months later showed an index of 2.91. The change in the record was not statistically significant. Despite overt clinical improvement at the time of the second record, this girl had another open psychotic break and had to be hospitalized in a closed institution several months later.

Not all psychotherapies work with the goal of lifting repression. In some cases the problem is one of reinforcing repressions. In an adult case treated by one of us, the presenting picture included a great deal of bizarre ideation, open homosexual fantasies, a general fantasy preoccupation, and a dramatic hysterical manner. The psychological examiner felt the patient was schizophrenic, and the psychiatric consultant supervising the case also felt there were borderline schizophrenic features in the patient. Therapy was suppressive, non-interpretive and supporting. The patient's attention was directed toward reality, and away from fantasies. After two years of treatment, the patient seemed more reality oriented, and for the first time in his life (he was then 30) held a job for more than three months. He was working for a year and a half at the time of reexamination. The pre-therapy RIRS was exceptionally high at 7.00. Following therapy, RIRS dropped to 2.83. This change is also highly significant by U test ($z = 3.18$; $p < .001$).

Not all successful psychotherapy cases show a shift in score. Harrower (1958) presents two cases, one in which psychoanalytically oriented psychotherapy was successful, and one in which brief psychotherapy had a successful outcome. In neither case did the index shift significantly. She also reports a number of unsuccessful cases, and in these the index remained almost identical on reexamination.

In individual cases, drug therapies also produce marked changes in psychological status. Henry Darmstadter, of Eugenia Hospital, Philadelphia, permitted us to see pre and post therapy records of a female schizophrenic patient who had been treated with massive doses of Thorazine and Serpasil with clinical improvement. In this case, the pre-therapy RIRS was 4.31, while the post-therapy RIRS was 1.95. This value was also statistically significant. In this case, the drug therapy had apparently resulted in increased repression.

The few cases are not presented to show that therapy results in personality change. The cases are presented to show one of the ways in which RIRS can be useful in appraising changes which occur in individual cases. One important element is the fact that the cases can be treated quantitatively, and a p value may be assigned to help assess the quantitative change.

CHANGE IN RIRS WITH CHANGE IN CLINICAL STATUS

Rorschach (1942) presents two records, one taken while the S was depressed, and one taken while the S was in a manic state. The RIRS for the depressed record was .75, while the RIRS for the manic state was 1.62. This difference between the two records is also statistically significant, by t test ($t = 3.48$; $p = .001$).

Beck (1945) presents a case study of a patient in hypomanic and in a depressed phase of his illness. The record in the hypomanic state yielded an RIRS of 6.70, while in the depressed period, the score dropped to 2.87. This difference in the two records was also highly significant statistically ($t = 4.16$; $p = .001$).

Beck (1945) presents another case study of a patient in psychosis and in remission. The record in psychosis yielded an RIRS of 4.36, while in remission RIRS was 4.28. In this instance change in the clinical status of the patient was not accompanied by change in RIRS. According to Beck's analysis of the record, other features do change, but the RIRS did not.

It is apparent that there are changes which occur which are not related to the RIRS score, and changes which are. RIRS is only one element of a record, and it is useful for what it is. There may come a time when we will understand the significance of such changes or lack of changes. For the present, it seems valuable to be able to represent an aspect of change in Rorschach performance by a single, simple quantitative index. Once again, the case studies are not meant to "validate" the index, but they are presented merely to indicate the score may reflect changes in clinical status, and that such changes may be assessed statistically, even in a single case.

SEQUENCE ANALYSIS OF RIRS

Among the other variables of interest in the Rorschach test is the sequence of responses. The sequence of location scores has always been of interest, but in more recent years, sequences of content, of determinants, and of response flow have received attention. Clinicians try to gauge such characteristics as "recoverability" from disturbance in response sequences. Phillips and Smith (1953) have presented a detailed view of various types of sequence analysis. They have pointed out the variety of cues the clinician integrates in forming his interpretative hypotheses.

The sequence of responses reflects the flow of the S's associations, and variations and shifts in the flow of associations may be taken to reflect something of the S's reactions to himself, his own thought products and to evaluations he perceives, or projects, in the examiner. RIRS may be employed to reveal variations in the associative flow during the course of a record. In this section, we present the free association portions of two Rorschach records.* In both tests, there is a distinctive shift in the quality of responses in different portions of the record. Both of these records have been scored for RIRS, and the purpose of this communication is

---

* These two cases were discussed in an article published in the *Journal of Projective Techniques* (1963, Vol. 27), and are reprinted here by permission of the publishers.

to demonstrate how the technique of scoring depicts the variations in response quality in quantitative fashion.

The first record is of a fifteen year old female who was a severe behavior problem and showed gross mistrust of herself and others. The numbers in parenthesis represent the weightings for the preceding terms. The value to the right is the score for that response.

			RIRS Response Total
I.	2″	LL two dancing (1) bears (1)	2
	6″	and a headless (1) woman (1)	2
II.	6″	Two headless (1) bears (1) fighting	
	19″	(3) with knives (2)	7
III.	2″	LL two monkeys (1) with bowling balls (1) or something	2
		These are either stomachs (2) or gall bladders (1) or something	3
	55″	And these are two stomachs (2)	2
IV.	3″	LL two boots (1). That's about all I can	
	11″	see	1
V.	16″	I don't know what this is. Doesn't LL anything. It doesn't LL anything	0
VI.	3″	This LL the head (0) of a cat (1) and that's about all	1
	18″	LL two little (1) birds (0) right here	1
VII.	3″	This LL two elves' (2) heads (0)	
	19″	That's all	2
VIII.	6″	Two wildcats (1). That's all	1
	17″		
IX.	4″	This doesn't remind me of anything	0
X.	9″	LL a devil's (2) head (0)	2
		and two dogs (0)	0
	45″	and two insects (0). That's about all	0

In this record the early aggressive and hostile content is followed by dependency symbols (the stomachs), and from that point on the associations become much more limited. The RIRS scores stay in the range 0-2, where earlier in the record, through card III, they were in the range 2-7. While rejecting some of the cards (scored 0, repressed), she speaks almost the same number of words throughout the test. She has a mean of approximately twelve words per card through card III, and a mean of about 11 words per card through the rest of the test. However, instead of communicating images and percepts in keeping with the instructions, her words serve to block the meaningful flow. There is a marked shift in the proportion of words which are "communicative" in terms of the test. The total verbal output does not change very much, but the RIRS for the first three cards is 3.00, while for the last seven cards, it is .80. It is not that she stops talking, or even that she talks less. It is simply that her communications become more "repressed." The distribution and sequence of the RIRS scores, response by response, seem to reflect a meaningful shift in her behavior during the testing situation. This case clearly indicates the distinction between a simple word count, as is sometimes used in analyzing TAT protocols (Webb and Hilden, 1953), and a count of the "communicative" terms in any verbal sample.

The second record was given by a twenty-two year old male, IQ 96, who has had diagnoses including inadequate personality, brain damage and pseudo-retardation. This record differs from the first in that the patient never rejects the cards. However, the relative richness of the responses changes quite drastically following a morbid response to card VIII.

			RIRS
			Response Total
I.	13″	LL a flying (1) eagle (1)	
	55″	That's all I know, it's a bird (0) of some kind	2
II.	6″	LL a chest (1) with a stomach (2), bone (0) broken (2)	5
	53″	or it could be an explosion (2)	2
III.	5″	LL two men (1) arguing (3) over a pot (1) of water (0)	5
	39″	(turns card frequently)	
IV.	4″	LL a gorilla (1) . . . that's it!	1
	27″	(puts card away)	
V.	19″	A bird (0) of some kind; I dk what you	0
	40″	call it; can't think right now	
VI.	13″	LL another explosion (2) coming out of the ground (1) . . .	3
	39″	Nothing else here! (puts card away)	
VII.	29″	LL inside of a cave . . . (1) walking (1)	2
	50″		
VIII.	23″	This LL . . . bears (1) working (1) on a dead (2) person's (0) chest (1);	
	58″	they are breaking (3) it up	8
IX.	16″	This up here LL witches (2)	2
		These things LL some kind of animals (0)	0
	72″	This LL mud (2)	2
X.	12″	This LL a wishing bone (1)	1
		These two LL some kind of a mountain (0)	0
		These LL fireworks (1)	1
		This LL a stump (1) of a tree (0)	1
		These two LL leaves (0)	0
	80″	This LL a fan (1) piece (0)	1

Card liked most: III; liked least: VIII (why?) "because
... oh ... I ... two bears working a chest, on a body, seems ...
wicked and scary."

There are several factors of interest in this record. The RIRS
scores vary from 0-8, but the mean for the first eight responses,
prior to card VIII is 2.50. The mean for nine responses following
card VIII is .89. The S continues to respond right through the
test, not rejecting any cards. However, once the morbid, hostile
image broke through, his manner of response changed quite drastically. If we followed the usual scores only, the shift in his response style might not be noted. Several of the later responses
contain movement and color determinants, as discovered in inquiry, and the VIII, IX, X per cent would be high. The RIRS
scores pick up the shift in the quality of the terms he uses in
expressing his responses, and depict the shift in quantitative
fashion.

A shift in style may also be seen earlier. Following the response to card III, which also contains hostile content, he gives
responses which score 0 and 1 to the next two cards. The disturbance in his behavior may be noted clinically. His behavior in
turning the card, his almost shouting "that's it!," the increasing
reaction times beginning with card V and his complaint on card
V that he cannot think, all reflect his disturbance following the
response on card III which also had hostile content.

From a clinical viewpoint, it may be added the patient com-
plains of "dizzy spells" which were not considered convulsive.
Neurological and EEG examinations were negative. The "dizzy
spells," which last five to ten minutes, may be episodes of "repression," but this is not definitely known.

The analysis provided by the RIRS scores indicated quantitatively what we may observe in the course of a detailed analysis
of the record. It is useful to note that the "communicative" value
of the terms of his responses changed, even though he continued
to respond throughout the test. The shift in his response style
is much more subtle than the shift noted in the previous record.
This S does not simply reject cards, but a quantitative analysis
of the terms of his response shows the change. He produced
fewer specific terms and fewer verbs.

Comparison of these two records also reveals at least two repressive styles in handling the total testing situation. In the girl's record, after hostile and oral images appear, there is a marked decrease in personalized imagery and affective verbalization throughout the remainder of the protocol. Once anxiety provoking material appeared, "repressive thinking" continued until the Rorschach situation ended. The man's record, on the other hand, reveals at least three instances (Cards II, III, VIII) when angry, and/or morbid imagery appears and is followed by an increase in repressive functioning and corresponding decrease in RIRS scores. The girl's record suggests an individual who, when anxious, becomes emotionally and personally removed from the total test situation. She does not permit any further personal commitment for some period of time, or at least until she is completely out of the situation. In the man's record, personal commitment varies within the total situation; withdrawal of personal material is temporary. S repeatedly becomes engaged and then "represses."

SUMMARY AND INTERPRETATION OF CLINICAL VALIDATION AND UTILITY DATA

1. RIRS differentiates significantly between textbook cases diagnosed as hysterics and cases diagnosed as obsessive compulsives. In accord with theory, hysterics produce lower RIRS scores, i.e., more repressed records, than obsessive compulsives. Limitations of this validation were indicated.

2. RIRS differentiates significantly between psychoneurotic and well functioning normal adult males. Normals produce less repressed records than psychoneurotics.

3. There is evidence that within the category of neurosis more repressed records are more likely to accompany an emphasis on somatic complaints, and less repressed records an emphasis on intra-psychic complaints. Patients with psychosomatic disorders in general produce more repressed records.

4. RIRS does not differentiate adolescent delinquents from other adolescent problems. However, there is some suggestive indication that male adolescents who act out sexually produce less repressed records than other delinquents.

5. Schizophrenics may have more repressed records than

other patient groups, but adequate controls to support this conclusion are not available.

6. Among schizophrenic women, verbal intelligence correlates quite highly with RIRS (approximately .60).

7. Schizophrenic women who required controls from ward
personnel and who were considered "active" had less repressed
records than patients who required stimulation and were considered passive.

8. There was some suggestive evidence that length of hospitalization in schizophrenic women may be related to the RIRS
score. Those with less repressed records tend to be discharged
sooner than those with more repressed records.

9. In view of the correlations of RIRS with intelligence, with
activity, with ability to report dreams and with tendency toward
earlier discharge, it is suggested that higher RIRS scores may
reflect greater psychological responsiveness in schizophrenic
women.

10. It is possible to evaluate changes in RIRS statistically in
individual cases. Individual case studies show statistically significant shifts in score in relation to various forms of psychotherapy, in relation to drug therapy and in relation to changes
in clinical status.

11. The usefulness of the RIRS score as a quantitative index
of variations in the flow of associations is demonstrated in two
records.

Chapter XII

THE INTERPRETIVE SIGNIFICANCE OF RIRS

In this chapter, we shall attempt to summarize some of our ideas concerning the significance of high and low RIRS scores. While we may write as if RIRS has a relatively constant meaning in any personality constellation, we recognize that its relatedness to specific overt behaviors may vary as a function of its interaction with other facets of a given personality. In what follows, we shall be guided by the various validity studies we have reported, but we shall include additional nuances of meaning which derive from clinical experience. The reader is cautioned that some of the statements come from the intensive observations of relatively few individuals whom we have come to know through psychotherapeutic and other clinical contacts. Also, our personal clinical experience is broader with males than with females and our comments may thereby be biased by this limitation in our experience. This chapter is an attempt to summarize our ideas. It is not meant to provide a cook book interpretation of an RIRS score.

THE "MEANING" OF RIRS

An RIRS score represents the extent to which an individual characteristically brings to bear his own thoughts, feelings and memories in organizing his experiences and giving meaning to his world. An RIRS score indicates the extent to which images, emotions and past experiences are verbally *labeled* and thus *available* in consciousness in *communicable terms*. Structurally, an RIRS score indicates the extent to which there is a *flowing* and *unbroken emergence of ideas* and *associations,* and the presence of *convergent lines of meaning* which yield multi-defined, specific ideas.

The data indicate that RIRS reflects an early developed and

stable stylistic feature of thinking and verbalization that has relevance to a wide range of behaviors.

SOME EXAMPLES OF HIGH AND LOW RIRS PEOPLE IN ACTION

In each example given below the first individual of the pair gave a low RIRS and the second a high RIRS score.

Imagine two people admiring the view of a dogwood tree in full bloom in the spring. One individual looks at it and remarks: "How beautiful!" A second individual looks at it and says, "It looks as if hundreds of white butterflies have landed on the tree."

A mother announces to two older children that they must give up the family dog because the baby of the family has developed a severe allergy, and the allergist believes he is sensitive to the dog. One child protests vehemently and immediately formulates a plan for building a doghouse in the backyard and keeping the dog outside. The second child responds equally vigorously, but the second child says the parents are getting rid of the dog because they don't like it, they don't want to take care of it, and because they don't like to see the children have fun.

An adolescent boy who is a behavior problem is enrolled in a residential treatment center. His response to the enrollment is negative because he feels he is blocked from doing as he pleases. A second boy is enrolled, and his feeling is also negative, but he feels the enrollment has stigmatized him, and has completely ruined his chances for entering a good college and making something of himself.

One adolescent boy came to his therapy hour furious. He had written a letter to his girl friend and he suspected that the residential school authorities had intercepted the letter, interfering with his relationship with the girl. The boy said he would see the girl anyway. An adult outpatient also came to his therapy hour in a rage. He suspected that his landlady had intercepted his mail and withheld a letter he was expecting from a girl friend because the landlady was trying to snare him for her own daughter. He had developed an elaborate scheme for mailing letters to a friend in California to be mailed from there so he could catch the landlady in the act.

One patient in therapy is asked, "But how is it that you became so angered by the remark?" His reply: "I don't know, it just made me mad!" A second patient is asked the same question and replies: "It seemed as if he was trying to belittle me, as if he didn't think very much of me."

One patient has obsessional fears of cancer, possible auditory hallucinations, severe attacks of anxiety approaching panic states and episodic outbreaks of a dermatitis thought to be psychosomatic in origin. This individual has put himself through music school, earns a living by teaching and playing, owns his own home and is investing in summer real estate. A second individual has at least a twenty point advantage in IQ over the first, but he is working as a relatively unskilled file clerk. He reported an incident in which he created much disruption and ill will in his office because he hounded every division manager to initial a memo stating that July 4th was an official holiday before he would file the memo in the permanent file for such documents. Technically he was absolutely correct in his insistence that all initial the memo, but his action was clearly motivated by his conscious fantasy that he was dominating the bosses and bending them to his will.

In each instance a similar circumstance produced a different mode of apprehending and experiencing the situation. In each example, the first individual, the low RIRS S, may be said to be in touch with the concrete, the practical or the "perceptual" realities of the situation, while the high RIRS S views the situation within a complex matrix of personal meanings and personal memories.

These features of experience inferred from behavior seem congruent with what is revealed about experience in the approach to the Rorschach blots. Just as the low RIRS S sticks closely to the inkblot—"It looks like an animal,"—so he sticks close to the events of his world. The high RIRS S interprets the world much as he does the blots. He imposes his own view and his own concerns, because his orientation has given him ready access to his storehouse of imagery.

The high RIRS S, less dependent upon outer stimulation, responds well to sensory isolation. He complies with the instructions to report all he experiences, and his rational thinking is not disrupted by the sensory isolation. In the rod and frame, the chair-window test (involving the mental manipulation of spatial characteristics), or in the leveling sharpening task, the high RIRS S is at an advantage. When an inner frame of reference is demanded by a situation, the high RIRS S meets this demand well. The experimental data and the clinical observations tend to support this general conclusion reasonably well. However, we would suspect that the high RIRS S would be at a disadvantage, relative to a low RIRS S, in situations in which it is necessary to respond to immediate perceptual "givens." For example, a twelve year old, high RIRS girl was very sensitive about her own feelings and desires relative to her peers and very shy. She very much wanted to make friends, and was hurt by frequent rejections. However, she could not realistically estimate why her peers rejected her, nor could she see them as different than herself in any way.

For the low RIRS, a situation seems to demand some action. There is perceptual reality, and a spontaneous tendency to manipulate the situation, to fight it or to turn away from it. The low RIRS seems to be a realist, or a pragmatist, although anxiety may lead him to adopt withdrawal or retreat as his most typical mode of response. The low RIRS may be said to be "issue" oriented. He acts because he has an end result to achieve in the world outside himself.

The high RIRS seems to be "cause" oriented. He is a "philosopher" and acts because his actions have meaning in a broader scheme of things. The specific goal he wants to achieve or the affect he wishes to avoid is good enough for the low RIRS. The high RIRS needs a "reason."

The difference between high and low RIRS may be likened to the difference (at least in the stereotypes we hold) between the "practical politician," and the "intellectual idealist." The practical politician may be willing to fight, to retreat, to compromise, depending upon his estimate of the vote getting potential of any action. The idealist has principles he will not compromise. A wrong is wrong, and evil will be exposed. Despite the realities, he speaks out for the "right."

Each in his own way may be very effective, and in given circumstances the actions of both may be the same, but the view and the basis for the actions may be entirely different. In one instance the activity is designed to achieve a definite and concrete aim. In the second it is as if the proper ideational categorization of an event is the most important consideration. The end result is less important than the feeling that the action is consistent with principle. For the high RIRS, situations have meaning in terms of personal memories, personal principles, and personal fantasies. For the low RIRS, situations have meaning in terms of more or less clearly visualized specific outcomes referred to the external world.

RIRS AND THE NATURE OF FANTASY

The fantasies of highs and lows tend to be different. Both may have very elaborate fantasies, but the low's fantasies will tend to be more impersonal in nature. He will think about doing things, and his fantasies will include himself as engaged in an activity. One low individual of modest intelligence had a fantasy of himself as a sports announcer. He would imagine himself announcing and reporting sporting events. He enjoyed every phase of athletics, and when he could, he lived out the fantasy by announcing school sporting events. Another low RIRS of high intelligence had the most elaborate "science fiction" fantasies. The fantasies usually included himself as participant, but his descriptions were occupied with the technical details of accomplishing faster than light flight, travel to other galaxies, the type of atmospheric conditions he would encounter, and the forms of life which might be there.

The fantasies of the high individual frequently have a much more narcissistic component. Achievement which might result in adulation of the self seems to be the content of such fantasies. The high RIRS focuses on himself more often in his fantasies. The content of the fantasy may vary but a central component is self-aggrandizement.

One high RIRS subject had the fantasy of earning $200 a week. This to him was the salary that a "real man" earned but he rarely thought or fantasied in any detail how he would earn the money.

Another high S fantasied himself as the center of attention in any group. If only he was given the chance, he could really "wow" the crowd. He could be a great public speaker, or a great philosopher who could sway men. But he seemed to want all this without any effort on his part in his fantasy. The precise nature of what he did was not as important as the fact that what he did in the fantasy would bring him glory.

The focus, in the fantasy of highs, upon self-aggrandizement is consistent with the correlation of n Ach and RIRS. The high individual's behavior in giving his Rorschach responses may be interpreted as reflecting both achievement motivation and a pride in exhibiting the products of his mind. When a subject gives a rich response, he is implicitly showing his achievement within a situation which requests that he respond fully to the instructions: "tell me what you see."

RIRS AND INNER CONFLICT

In keeping with the implications of free-flowing thinking, a subject high in RIRS is likely to have an awareness of contradictions and conflicts in himself. If he overvalues himself in narcissistic fashion, he is also aware of striking feelings of inferiority at the same time. He frequently vacillates between an inflated self image which follows from a fantasied overevaluation of given achievements, and a deflated self image, following upon equally elaborate fantasies stimulated by rebuffs or defeats.

An individual low in RIRS may suffer from the same kind of conflicts, but the two elements of the conflict are usually not in awareness. If there is overevaluation of the self, or some degree of grandiosity, then the feeling of inferiority is rarely expressed, or experienced only as a tension state. In the same way, if the sense of inadequacy is prominent in an individual low in RIRS, the conflicting wish for achievement, or the implicity held demand for super-attainment is usually unconscious (in the sense that the clinician may infer it from the patient's attitudes) and the patient will not usually be willing or able to verbalize the desire for achievement.

Awareness of both sides of a conflict situation is consistent with a general tendency in high RIRS to see various possibilities in a new situation. Such individuals can take various perspectives and see various alternative forms of action that might be taken. Whether such mental "fluency" leads to creative and original solutions or mere obsessional doubting and indecision is another question.

RIRS AND PARANOID AND OBSESSIONAL IDEATION

Similarly, paranoid ideation, when it is an element in the personality, differs in high and low RIRS Ss. The low RIRS S will have a simple, unelaborated delusion. Others are calling him a homosexual, or he has a sense of being disliked, but elaborate plots do not seem to be developed by the low RIRS. In contrast high RIRS Ss will find elaborate reasons for the persecutions they project. One such schizophrenic adult described himself as a vacation patient in a hospital where the doctors and nurses were constantly exposing him to sexual temptations so that he would break down and agree to get married. An outpatient described the EEG as a device which would tell the doctor whether he was crazy, and this information would then give the doctor enormous power over him.

The content of obsessional thoughts also differs in a similar dimension. A low RIRS patient would be concerned that he had cancer every time he noticed a pimple or other blemish on his face. When his wife was late for an appointment, he had the simple thought she had been hit by a car. Another low RIRS patient would find himself beset with an obscene thought when with wives of his friends. However, the thought was a bare idea without additional fantasy elaboration.

Obsessional-like thinking in high RIRS patients takes on the character of ruminations continuing over long periods of time and becoming highly elaborated. A fancied slight is mulled over and developed until it becomes a major incident. A high RIRS patient had the thought every once in a while that he would somehow change into a woman, but the thought did not stop at this. He would think how this would happen and develop elaborate scientific explanations involving elements from various Sunday supplements. At times he would experience some tinge of fear that it was possible he would change into a woman.

While obsessive compulsive patients seem to produce records with relatively high scores, some will produce rather long records with many simple, unelaborated responses. Obsessive and compulsive characteristics are notable in such individuals, but it is our hypothesis that details of the obsessional ideas will be different depending on the RIRS score.

RIRS AND AFFECT DISCHARGE

Our reliability studies have shown that various circumstances (e.g., instructional set) can shift the mean level of RIRS scores. However, despite these shifts in mean, the relative ordering of the Ss, as reflected in correlation coefficients, remains fairly constant from condition to condition, and through time. From the fact that the style is relatively constant while the mean level of score shifts, we may deduce that more is involved in high RIRS scores than simply the willingness and ability to respond fully. The S must have a mental "apparatus" which permits the ready flow of ideation. S somehow must permit himself to "think," or at least he must have areas of thought in which anxiety, or avoidance responses do not shut off the flow of thought. Confirming Dollard and Miller's (1950) theoretical view, Eriksen and Keuthe (1956) have shown that "pain" can result in the avoidance of thought.

The high RIRS S (at least the male), may be sufficiently anxiety free, or tolerant of anxiety, so that he can permit his mind to roam freely, wherever the associations take him. Either he does not have the same level of anxiety or, paradoxically, words which seem to be so important in his dynamic structure are relatively isolated from affect. It may be that since the high RIRS S does think in relatively specific and precise terms, as we gather from his words, small quantities of affect are associated with the precise term, and his affective reactions may be described as more differentiated and modulated in intensity.

Some examples may serve. In therapy, a low RIRS S was confronted in a clumsy and untimely way with a depth interpretation. The patient's reaction was one of near panic. He slumped back in his seat, the color and energy almost visibly draining from him. His reaction was a very complete one. Another low RIRS individual came exceedingly close to facing his murderous feelings toward his wife and children in a therapy hour. The patient returned two days later reporting that he had been in a continuous state of anxiety verging on panic. A third low RIRS patient would frequently be subjected to abuse by a superior. Typically, he woud be unaware of the abuse as such, but he would promptly develop a headache. On two occasions following provoking experiences, the patient awoke from his sleep with choking reactions, and feelings of panic. The affective reactions in these individuals were prompt, intense and diffuse.

In contrast, a high RIRS S, probably a borderline schizophrenic but not overtly homosexual, reported that during his time in service he had suddenly experienced conscious fellatio fantasies, had been very anxious about these, but managed to "sit" on the anxiety without any marked disruption of his everyday behavior.

A second high RIRS S, who was being stimulated by an older, sexually provocative and somewhat promiscuous woman who also served him as a mother figure, considered the oedipal implications of his situation with some degree of disturbance, but several days later there was no longer any indication that the discussion continued to disturb him.

A third high RIRS S, an adolescent, was able to some extent to alleviate a depressed mood precipitated by his father's leaving to go on a business trip by associating the feeling to his concerns about abandonment and his fears that he was unable to depend on a very erratic mother.

In other words, the high RIRS Ss were able to deal with what we ordinarily conceive as "depth material" without being entirely overwhelmed by the material. All of these high Ss were anxious, and all had symptoms of various kinds. In his own way, each was as disturbed as the several low RIRS described above, but each was able to tolerate and deal with ideas which were extremely disruptive to the low RIRS Ss.

We suspect that the high S has more cognitive "tools" with which to regulate and channelize tension. Rapaport (1951) argues that the delay of tension discharge and the development of ego controls are predicated upon the development of hierarchical thought processes which offer partial channels of discharge and which neutralize drive tension. Having available a highly active and differentiated cognitive apparatus, the high RIRS person can bind and deploy tensions, tolerate postponement and delay of gratification, and construct more subtle defensive maneuvers than the low RIRS individual. The latter should suffer from diffuse tension discharge, vague anxieties, and somatic complaints more frequently. Perhaps the high RIRS can manifest a more focused or "insightful" handling of affect because for him it is only a partial discharge, and he is capable of binding and/or neutralizing remaining tension.

RIRS AND ACTION

Despite the fact that high RIRS Ss seem to engage rather freely in loose, and even wild thinking, the wild and loose thinking is not likely to express itself in equivalently wild actions (except perhaps in schizophrenic women). The overt behavior of the high RIRS S (the male particularly), is likely to be much more limited and deliberate, although in given instances the behavior may appear impulsive or unwarranted by circumstances.

There is a joke about a man who found himself stranded on a lonely road in the middle of the night, his car having a flat tire, and he without a working jack. A long way down the road, the man saw the lights of what might be a service station. He began walking toward the light, and as he was walking, he thought of his situation. He felt a momentary relief that a service station was so close at hand, but then he began thinking of what the service might cost him. At first, he thought the service man could not charge him more than a dollar or two, but then the thought came that it was the middle of the night, and he was stuck. The anticipated price went up, and as the price went up in his imagination so did his indignation at being cheated. When he finally arrived at the service station, he flung open the door, and shouted angrily at the bewildered service station attendant: "Keep your jack at those prices!!"

One high RIRS S mulled over and elaborated his grievances in fantasy for weeks until he finally decided to tell off the boss. He obtained an appointment, reeled off a list of real and fancied gripes, and almost quit his job. An adolescent with high RIRS who felt himself tormented by schoolmates over a period of some weeks reported that calmly and deliberately, and without warning, he walked up to one of his tormenters and punched him. In contrast, an adolescent who had low RIRS impulsively struck a little girl who was a complete stranger to him, because he felt she was "nagging" him. Then, in a panic that he would be caught, he ran to a nearby wooded area, dragging and carrying the little girl by the neck, choking her to death.

The high RIRS S will act, but his action is more likely to be a deliberate, a focused and a partial response, rather than a diffuse, impulsive, unthinking reflex-like response. It is more likely that interposed between stimulus and response are a chain of thoughts, or means-ends considerations. The correlations of RIRS with *M* enable us to identify RIRS with the body of research on processes related to the delay of gratification (Singer, 1960).

RIRS IN FEMALES

Some of our data suggest that correlates of RIRS in females are different in some respects than in males. In contrast to men, normal women with high RIRS tend to make more extreme and rapid judgments when using the semantic differential scales than low RIRS women. Also, in contrast to high RIRS men, high RIRS females report more symptoms of anxiety and personal problems, show high self-ideal discrepancy scores, and respond to a vocational interest questionnaire with less consistent choices than a comparison group of low RIRS females (see Chapter X).

Clinical observation of a few cases of high and low RIRS women and girls fills out some of the suggestions of the more formal studies. Two pairs of sisters, one pair adult and one pair children, had markedly different Rorschachs, one of each pair giving relatively low scores. The two adults were normals, studied as part of a research project in family life and child rearing.* The two children were living at home but were brought by their parents for clinical evaluation because of some problems each was having.

The low RIRS adult sister was specifically characterized both

---

* This project was under the direction of Guinivere Chambers, of the University of Pittsburgh Medical School.

by the interviewer and by her sister as tending to minimize and deny personal problems. The high RIRS sister, for example, complained the other would never intimately discuss personal problems with her, while the low RIRS sister stated she rarely had periods of anxiety or depression. Of the two children, the low RIRS sister was brought for evaluation after she had developed convulsions at about age ten. When seen for testing, she had a strong need to deny the illness, or the seriousness of it. She refused to let it interfere with her actions in any way at all, and used euphemistic expressions to describe her seizures.

In contrast, the high RIRS adult saw the research interview as a personal "psychoanalysis" and discussed problems she was having with her husband quite openly. The high RIRS child was seen for examination because of a developing problem of obesity. Although initially reluctant to talk about her eating, once she did, she made it clear she had no conflict about her desire to eat, her "stealing" of food, or her temper tantrums when denied candy and other fattening foods. Of the two children, the mother found the high RIRS child the more tractable, except in this one respect of eating, and yet of the two, the high RIRS sister was the one who gave the mother the greater cause for worry. The two high RIRS females somehow seemed to let their worries come more to the surface so that problems were readily noticeable.

Clinical observation also suggests that the low RIRS female may be the more competent in dealing with her life situation. In comparing the two adults, it was observed the home and living conditions of the low RIRS sister were better organized than in the home of the high RIRS sister. The low RIRS subject had much greater system in her life, she was firmer with her children, almost compulsively active in her community and she was active with her husband in their own business. In contrast, the high RIRS sister did not seem to have her home under the same kind of directed and systematic control, and her children were less well behaved in the conventional sense, although they were by no means behavior problems.

Similarly, of the two children, the low RIRS sister was much more physically active, much more athletically inclined, and constantly involved in projects involving the manipulation of materials. The high RIRS sister, in contrast, was relatively inactive physically, exceedingly slow to express any kind of aggression, and while having some artistic talent, she was usually content to amuse herself quietly rather than do, and show off her products. The purposefulness, the force and the direction of the low RIRS sisters is in direct contrast to the relative passivity of the high RIRS sisters.

The high RIRS female may be less "practical" in her handling of everyday problems and thus less competent in her "role." We would hypothesize that this is also true of males, in the sense that the high RIRS male is less oriented to the practical consequences of possible actions than to the "meaning" actions have in the sense of "rightness." However, in contrast to females, high RIRS males report, and presumably experience, *less* anxiety and personal problems, and are *more* focused in their performance. High RIRS males seem more capable of putting off gratification, high RIRS females seem less so, and the passivity in high RIRS women seems to express a gross self-indulgence. It is of interest that schizophrenic women who have high RIRS scores are rated as more *active*. The schizophrenic condition may modify the significance of the RIRS score. There is much room for investigation of these sex differences in personality structure. Our own limited results on sex differences do not yet permit the development of an articulated point of view.

SUMMARY

This research began with the clinical observation that individuals differ greatly in the extent of verbal development of responses to inkblots. A scoring system designed to highlight and to measure the extent of verbal development of the responses proved to be workable. The measure itself proved to be reliable under a variety of tests. From the extensive evaluation of the consistency of the measure, we can safely conclude the behavior under study is an early evolved stylistic property of language (and presumably thought) and is relatively stable over long periods of time.

As a working conception, we think of RIRS as a measure of verbal output from which one can infer a style of thinking. We initially adopted the name "repressive style" for two reasons. The modifier "repressive" is justified on the grounds that we are dealing with a measure of the use of words in describing percepts. In operational terms (Freud, 1915a; Dollard and Miller, 1950; Madison, 1960), it can be argued that an act of repression is manifested, at least in part, by a failure of appropriate labels (i.e., words) to appear in consciousness. The label "style" is used to convey the conception that the behavior we measure is not limited to a single act. A specific act of repression may be observed in psychotherapy, or in a laboratory situation, but we think of a style as reflecting a more general characteristic of behavior. The term *style* suggests that we are dealing with some quality of a function. The function is operative in a wide variety of circumstances, and the quality can be noted in the total response to a variety of situations that call upon the function.

We are dealing with the language employed in giving Rorschach responses. If language is limited (in the way in which we define the RIRS score), then we infer that the underlying thought process also has certain gross limits. If the language is fuller and more elaborate, then we infer that the underlying thought process is also fuller and more elaborate. We have used the term "repressive" to signify this gross limitation of the thought process. This concept of repression has served as a guide in our research, and as a guide it had a certain usefulness. Several hypotheses derived from this meaning of RIRS have been supported.

However, the terms "repressive style" may place too stringent a limit on the kind of theoretical thinking one might do. At this point in its development, we would prefer to think of RIRS as a shorthand notation for one kind of score from the Rorschach record. The theoretical meaning of RIRS is given by the conception that an RIRS score represents the degree to which an individual characteristically brings "inner processes" to bear in organizing experience and in giving meaning to his world. Those high in RIRS, we would argue, reveal a greater availability of internal responses which can be put into language. Having a greater availability of words for emotions, motives, memories and fantasies, the current stimulating circumstances will be verbally labeled and categorized to a greater extent. The higher degree of accessibility to verbal labeling permits the high RIRS individual to be less dependent upon immediate stimulating circumstances for his response. He is more likely to respond in terms of his set of verbal labels than to the specific structural characteristics of a given situation. Because his language is full, we argue that his set of verbal labels will be used to mediate finer discriminations among stimulating circumstances. Given finer discrimination, responses should be more focused and partial, and less total and generalized. In general we expect greater self control from high RIRS individuals. As a further consequence of the tendency to respond in terms of the personal labeling, it might be expected that the high RIRS individual would be at a disadvantage in circumstances which require reflexive-like action to the immediate present. If a direct action solution is available, it would be expected that the individual low in RIRS would be better able to produce such a solution.

In general, low RIRS scores seem to go along with the presence of psychopathology, but psychopathology may be a relatively independent dimension from RIRS, and the interpretation of an RIRS score may have to be modified depending upon the "normal" or psychopathological context of the record. Low RIRS scores may go along with either heightened impulsivity or generalized constriction accompanied by diffuse, internal discharge of affect, and perhaps by psychosomatic symptoms. Individuals high in RIRS may be less well organized personally, less "practical" in everyday affairs, and more likely to be fantasy ridden or self-preoccupied. Also, there are notable sex differences in the significance of RIRS scores, and these should be kept firmly in mind in research or clinical uses of RIRS.

RIRS is a working instrument. We suspect that its greatest uses will be in research efforts initially, and hopefully research will lead to a greater understanding of this tool. The theoretical base of RIRS is hardly developed, but by attempting to tie the measure to verbal mediation theory, we hope to tie behavior measured in projective tests to general psychological theory. Hopefully, advances in theory may be used to sharpen testing procedures, and the findings from testing procedures may have theoretical significance.

BIBLIOGRAPHY

Altrocchi, J., Parsons, O. A., and Dickoff, Hilda: Changes in self-ideal discrepancy in repressors and sensitizers. *J. abn. soc. Psychol.*, 61:67-72, 1960.

Ames, Louise B., Learned, J., Metraux, Ruth W., and Walker, R. N.: *Child Rorschach Responses*. New York, Hoeber-Harper, 1952.

Ames, Louise B., Metraux, Ruth W., and Walker, R. N.: *Adolescent Rorschach Responses*. New York, Hoeber-Harper, 1959.

Barratt, E. S.: The space-visualization factors related to temperament traits. *J. Psychol.*, 39:279-287, 1955.

Barthol, R. P.: Individual and sex differences in cortical conductivity. *J. Pers.*, 26:365-378, 1958.

Beck, S. J.: *Rorschach's Test*. Vol. I. Basic processes. New York, Grune and Stratton, 1944.

Beck, S. J.: *Rorschach's Test*. Vol. II. A variety of personality pictures. New York, Grune and Stratton, 1945.

Beck, S. J., Beck, Anne G., Levitt, E. E., and Molish, H. B.: *Rorschach's Test*. I. Basic processes. 3rd Ed. Rev. New York, Grune and Stratton, 1961.

Beloff, H.: Two forms of social conformity: acquiescence and conventionality. *J. abn. soc. Psychol.*, 56:99-104, 1958.

Berdie, R. F.: Range of interests. *J. appl. Psychol.*, 29:268-281, 1945.

Berdie, R. F.: Range of interests and psychopathologies. *J. clin. Psychol.*, 2:161-166, 1946.

Bochner, Ruth, and Halpern, Florence: *The Clinical Application of the Rorschach Test*. New York, Grune and Stratton, 1942.

Byrne, D.: The repression-sensitization scale: rationale, reliability, and validity. *J. Pers.*, 29:334-349, 1961.

Campbell, Frances A., and Fiddleman, P. B.: The effect of examiner status upon Rorschach performance. *J. proj. Tech.*, 23:303-306, 1959.

Carlson, E. R., and Carlson, Rae: Male and female subjects in personality research. *J. abn. soc. Psychol.*, 61:482-483, 1960.

Cattell, R. B.: The principal replicated factors discovered in objective personality tests. *J. abn. soc. Psychol.*, 50:291-314, 1955.

Cattell, R. B., and Scheier, I. H.: *The Meaning and Measurement of Neuroticism and Anxiety*. New York, Ronald Press, 1961.

Cliff, N.: Adverbs as multipliers. *Psychol. Rev.*, 66:27-44, 1959.

DeVos, G.: A quantitative approach to affective symbolism in Rorschach responses. *J. proj. Tech.*, 16:133-150, 1952.

Dollard, J., and Miller, N. E.: *Personality and Psychotherapy.* New York, McGraw-Hill, 1950.

Due, F. O., and Wright, M. E.: The use of content analysis in Rorschach interpretation. I. Differential characteristics of male homosexuals. *Ror. Res. Exch.*, 9:169-177, 1945.

Eichman, W. J.: Replicated factors on the MMPI with female NP patients. *J. consult. Psychol.*, 25:55-60, 1961.

Elizur, A.: Content analysis of the Rorschach with regard to anxiety and hostility. *Ror. Res. Exch., & J. proj. Tech.*, 13:247-284, 1949.

Eriksen, C. W.: Personality. *Annu. Rev. Psychol.*, 8:185-210, 1957.

Eriksen, C. W., and Davids, A.: The meaning and clinical validity of the Taylor anxiety scale and the hysteria-psychasthenia scales from the MMPI. *J. abnorm. soc. Psychol.*, 50:135-137, 1955.

Eriksen, C. W., and Kuethe, J. L.: Avoidance conditioning of verbal behavior without awareness: a paradigm of repression. *J. abnorm. soc. Psychol.*, 53:203-209, 1956.

Ford, Mary: *The Application of the Rorschach Test to Young Children.* Minneapolis, University of Minnesota Press, 1946.

Framo, J. L., Osterweil, J., and Boszormenyi-Nagy, I.: A relationship between threat in the manifest content of dreams and active-passive behavior in psychotics. *J. abn. soc. Psychol.*, 65:41-47, 1962.

Freud, S. (1915a): Repression. In the *Complete Psychological Works of Sigmund Freud*, Vol. 14, London, Hogarth, 1957.

Freud, S. (1915b): The unconscious. In the *Complete Psychological Works of Sigmund Freud*, Vol. 14, London, Hogarth, 1957.

Gardner, R., Holzman, P. S., Klein, G. A., Linton, Harriet, and Spence, D. P.: Cognitive control: a study of individual consistencies in cognitive behavior. *Psychol. Issues, 1*, No. 4, 1959.

Harrower, Molly R.: *Personality Change and Development.* New York, Grune and Stratton, 1958.

Harrower, Molly R.: New developments in the Rorschach Technique. Paper read on a symposium at the meeting of the Eastern Psychol. Assn., Atlantic City, April, 1959.

Harrower-Erickson, M. R., and Steiner, M. E.: *Large Scale Rorschach Techniques: a Manual for the Group Rorschach and Multiple Choice Test.* Springfield, Thomas, 1945.

Heilbrun, Alfred B.: The psychological significance of the MMPI K scale in a normal population. *J. consult. Psychol.*, 25:486-491, 1961.

Hemmendinger, L.: Developmental theory and the Rorschach Method. In Maria A. Rickers-Ovsiankina, (Ed.) *Rorschach Psychology.* New York, Wiley, 1960.

Herskovitz, H. H., Levine, M., and Spivack, G.: Anti-social behavior of adolescents from higher socio-economic groups. *J. nerv. ment. Dis.*, 125:467-476, 1959.

Hertzman, M., and Pearce, J.: The personal meaning of the human figure in the Rorschach. *Psychiatry*, 10:413-422, 1947.

Hilgard, E. R.: *Theories of Learning.* 2nd Ed. New York, Appleton-Century-Crofts, 1956.

Hillson, J. S., and Worchel, P.: Self concept and defensive behavior in the maladjusted. *J. consult. Psychol.*, *21*:83-88, 1957.

Holt, R. R., and Goldberger, L.: Personological correlates of reactions to perceptual isolation. *WADC Techn. Rep.*, 59-735, 1959.

Holt, R. R., and Havel, Joan: A Method for Assessing Primary and Secondary Process in the Rorschach. In Maria A. Rickers-Ovsiankina (Ed.), *Rorschach Psychology*. New York, John Wiley & Sons, 1960.

Holtzman, W. H., Thorpe, J. S., Swartz, J. D., and Heron, E. W.: *Inkblot Perception and Personality: Holtzman Inkblot Technique*. Austin, Texas, Univer. Texas Press, 1961.

Holzberg, J. D.: Reliability Re-examined. In Maria A. Rickers-Ovsiankina (Ed.) *Rorschach Psychology*. New York, John Wiley & Sons, 1960, 361-379.

Holzman, P. S.: Repression and Cognitive Style. In J. G. Peatman and E. L. Hartley (Eds.) *Festschrift for Gardner Murphy*. New York, Harpers, 330-343, 1960.

Holzman, P. S., and Gardner, R. W. Leveling and repression. *J. abnorm. soc. Psychol.*, *59*:151-155, 1959.

Honigfeld, G., and Spigel, I. M.: Achievement motivation and field independence. *J. consult. Psychol.*, *24*:550-551, 1960.

Jensen, A. R.: The reliability of projective techniques. Review of the literature. *Acta Psychol.*, *16*:3-67, 1959.

Klopfer, B., Ainsworth, Mary D., Klopfer, W. G., and Holt, R. R.: *Developments in the Rorschach Technique*. Vol. I. *Technique and Theory*. Yonkers-on-Hudson, World Book Co., 1954.

Klopfer, B., and Kelley, D. M.: *The Rorschach Technique*. Yonkers-on-Hudson, World Book Co., 1942.

Kogan, N.: Authoritarianism and repression. *J. abn. soc. Psychol.*, *53*:34-37, 1956.

Kramer, A.: A Quick Rank Test for Significance of Differences in Multiple Comparisons. *Food Techn.*, *10*:391-392, 1956.

Lachman, F. M., Lapkin, B., and Handleman, N. S.: The recall of dreams: Its relation to repression and cognitive control. *J. abn. soc. Psychol.*, *64*:160-162, 1962.

Ledwith, Nettie H.: *Rorschach Responses of Elementary School Children: A Normative Study*. Pittsburgh, Univ. of Pittsburgh Press, 1959.

Levine, M., Spivack, G., and Wight, B.: The inhibition process, Rorschach human movement responses and intelligence: some further data. *J. consult. Psychol.*, *23*:306-312, 1959.

Levitt, E. E., and Grosz, H. J.: A comparison of quantifiable Rorschach anxiety indicators in hypnotically induced anxiety and normal states. *J. consult. Psychol.*, *24*:31-34, 1960.

Lindner, R. M.: Content analysis in Rorschach work. *Ror. Res. Exch.*, *10*: 121-129, 1946.

Loveland, Nathene T., and Thaler-Singer, Margaret: Projective test assessment of the effects of sleep deprivation. *J. proj. techn.*, *23*:323-334, 1959.

Luria, A. R.: *The Role of Speech in the Regulation of Normal and Abnormal Behavior*. New York, Liveright, 1961.

Madison, P.: *Freud's Concept of Repression and Defense, Its Theoretical and Observational Language.* Minneapolis, Univ. Minn. Press, 1961.

McClelland, D. C.: Methods of Measuring Human Motivation. In J. W. Atkinson (Ed.) *Motives in Fantasy, Action and Society.* Princeton, Van Nostrand, 1958.

McClelland, D. C., Atkinson, J. W., Clark, R. A., and Lowell, E. L.: *The Achievement Motive.* New York: Appleton-Century-Crofts, 1953.

Munroe, Ruth L.: The Inspection Technique for the Rorschach Protocol. In L. A. Abt, and L. Bellak (Eds.) *Projective Psychology.* New York, Alfred A. Knopf, 1950.

Murphy, G.: *Personality.* New York, Harpers, 1947.

Noyes, A. P.: *Modern Clinical Psychiatry.* Philadelphia, Saunders, 1953 (Fourth Ed.).

Osgood, C. E.: *Method and Theory in Experimental Psychology.* New York, Oxford Univ. Press, 1953.

Osgood, C. E., Suci, G. J., and Tannenbaum, P. H.: *The Measurement of Meaning.* Urbana, Univ. of Illinois Press, 1957.

Page, H. A.: Studies in fantasy: Daydreaming frequency and Rorschach scoring categories. *J. consult. Psychol., 21:*111-114, 1957.

Page, H. A.: Studies in fantasy, daydreaming and the TAT. *Amer. Psychologist, 11:*392 (abstract), 1956.

Paulsen, Alma A.: Personality development in the middle years of childhood. *Amer. J. Orthopsychiat., 24:*336-350, 1954.

Phillips, L., and Smith, J. G.: *Rorschach Interpretation: Advanced Technique.* New York, Grune and Stratton, 1953.

Piotrowski, Z. A.: *Perceptanalysis.* New York, Macmillan, 1957.

Piotrowski, Z. A.: The prognostic possibilities of the Rorschach method in insulin treatment. *Psychiat. Quart., 12:*679-689, 1938.

Piotrowski, Z. A.: The Rorschach inkblot method in organic disturbances of the central nervous system. *J. nerv. Ment. Dis., 86:*525-537, 1937.

Powers, W. T., and Hamlin, R. M.: Relationship between diagnostic category and deviant verbalizations on the Rorschach. *J. consult. Psychol., 14:*120-124, 1955.

Rapaport, D.: *Organization and Pathology of Thought.* New York, Columbia Univ. Press, 1951.

Rapaport, D.: The theory of ego autonomy: A generalization. *Bull. Menninger Clin., 22:*13-35, 1958.

Rapaport, D., Gill, M., and Schafer, R.: *Diagnostic Psychological Testing.* Vol. II. Chicago, Year Book Publishers, 1946.

Rogers, C.: *Client Centered Therapy.* Boston, Houghton Mifflin, 1951.

Rohrer, J. H., Hoffman, E. L., Bagby, J. W., Jr., Hermann, R. S., and Wilkins, W. L.: The group administered Rorschach as a research instrument: Reliability and norms. *Psychol. Monogr., 69:* Whole No. 393, 1955.

Rorschach, H.: *Psychodiagnostics: A Diagnostic Test Based on Perception.* Bern, Hans Huber, 1942.

Rothaus, P., and Worchel, P.: The inhibition of aggression under nonarbitrary frustration. *J. Pers., 28:*108-117, 1960.

Sarason, S. B.: *The Clinical Interaction: with Special Reference to the Rorschach.* New York, Harper and Bros., 1954.

Sarason, S. B., Davidson, K. S., Lighthall, F. F., Waite, R. R., and Ruebush, B. K.: *Anxiety in Elementary School Children.* New York, John Wiley & Sons, 1960.

Schachtel, E. G.: Subjective definitions of the Rorschach test situation and their effect on test performance. Contributions to an understanding of Rorschach's test. III. *Psychiatry, 8:*419-448, 1945.

Schafer, R.: *The Clinical Application of Psychological Tests.* New York, International Univ. Press, 1948.

Schafer, R.: *Psychoanalytic Interpretation in Rorschach Testing: Theory and Application.* New York, Grune and Stratton, 1954.

Schonbar, Rosalea A.: Temporal and emotional factors in the selective recall of dreams. *J. consult. Psychol., 25:*67-73, 1961.

Schwartz, F., and Kates, S. L.: Rorschach performance, anxiety level and stress. *J. proj. Tech., 21:*154-160, 1957.

Siegel, S.: *Nonparametric Statistics for the Behavioral Sciences.* New York, McGraw-Hill, 1956.

Singer, J. L.: The Experience Type: Some Behavioral Correlates and Theoretical Implications. In Maria A. Rickers-Ovsiankina (Ed.), *Rorschach Psychology.* New York, John Wiley and Sons, 1960, pp. 223-259.

Singer, J. L., and Herman, J. L.: Motor and fantasy correlates of Rorschach human movement responses. *J. consult. Psychol., 18:*325-331, 1954.

Singer, J. L., and Schonbar, Rosalea A.: Correlates of daydreaming: A dimension of self awareness. *J. consult. Psychol., 25:*1-6, 1961.

Singer, J. L., Wilensky, H., and McCraven, Vivian G.: Delaying capacity, fantasy and planning ability: A factorial study of some basic ego functions. *J. consult. Psychol., 20:*375-383, 1956.

Spivack, G., Levine, M., and Brenner, B.: Sex, verbal style and the use of the semantic differential. Report to Natl. Inst. Hlth., Research Grant No. M-4041, 1961.

Spivack, G., and Levine, M.: Note on the relationship between figural after-effects and intelligence in diffusely brain damaged individuals. *Percept. & Mot. Sk., 13:*342, 1961.

Steiner, I. D.: Sex differences in the resolution of A-B-X conflicts. *J. Pers., 28:*118-128, 1960.

Thurstone, L. L.: *A Factorial Study of Perception.* Chicago, Univ. Chicago Press, 1944.

Trier, T. R.: Vocabulary as a basis for estimating intelligence from the Rorschach. *J. consult. Psychol., 22:*289-291, 1958.

Tuddenham, R. D.: Correlates of yielding to a distorted group norm. *J. Pers., 27:*272-284, 1959.

Watkins, J., and Stauffacher, J.: An index of pathological thinking. *J. proj. Tech., 16:*272-286, 1952.

Webb, W. B., and Hilden, A. H.: Verbal and intellectual ability as factors in projective test results. *J. proj. Tech., 17:*102-103, 1953.

Weiner, L., Brown, E., and Kaplan, B.: A comparison of the ability of normals and brain injured subjects to produce additional responses on a second administration of the Rorschach test. *J. clin. Psychol., 12:*89-91, 1956.

Weisskopf-Joelson, Edith: A transcendence index as a proposed measure in the TAT. *J. Psychol., 29:*379-390, 1950.

Weisskopf-Joelson, Edith, Asher, E. J., Albrecht, K. J., and Hoffman, M. L.:
An experimental investigation of "label avoidance" as a manifestation
of repression. *J. proj. Tech.*, 21:88-93, 1957.

Welsh, G. S., and Dahlstrom, W. G. (Eds.): *Basic Readings on the MMPI
in Psychology and Medicine.* Minneapolis, Univer. Minn. Press, 1956.

Wheeler, W. M.: An analysis of Rorschach indices of male homosexuality.
J. proj. Tech., 13:97-126, 1949.

Wiggins, J. S.: Strategic, method and stylistic variance in the MMPI. *Psychol.
Bull.*, 59:224-242, 1962.

Witkin, H. A., Lewis, H. B., Hertzman, M., Machover, Karen, Neissner, P.
B., and Wapner, S.: *Personality Through Perception.* New York, Harper,
1954.

Wohlwill, J. F.: Developmental studies of perception. *Psychol. Bull.*, 57:249-
288, 1960.

Worchel, P.: Adaptability screening of flying personnel: Development of
a self-concept inventory for predicting maladjustment. SAM, USAF,
Randolph AFB, Texas, No. 56-62, 1957.

Young, H. H.: A test of Witkin's field-dependence hypothesis. *J. abnorm.
soc. Psychol.*, 59:188-192, 1959.

Zax, M., Stricker, G., and Weiss, J. R.: Some effects of non-personality
factors on Rorschach performance. *J. proj. Tech.*, 24:83-93, 1960.

Zeller, A. F. An experimental analogue of repression. II. Historical summary.
Psychol. Bull., 47:39-51, 1950.

APPENDIX

THIS APPENDIX presents the medians, the interquartile ranges and the ranges of RIRS scores for samples we have had occasion to study. The method of selection of Ss, the Ns and techniques of administering the tests may vary from sample to sample, and the samples are by no means comparable. The data are presented more for the guidance of other workers. They are not meaningful norms. The data are also presented in terms of medians and interquartile ranges because distributions are frequently skewed, and the standard deviations would not be completely meaningful. The interquartile range offers a simple unambiguous view of the middle range of scores. More precise percentile norms are not warranted by the types of data we have.

Those working with children will find several sets of data at many of the age levels, and the scores and distributions are not always precisely comparable. One sample is Ledwith's and the other was obtained from the Gesell Institute. The reader is referred to Chapter VI (Developmental Trends) for a discussion of the differences between these two samples.

Experienced Rorschach workers do not need this caution, but for novices, it cannot be emphasized too strongly that one *cannot* diagnose psychopathology with the RIRS score alone. Even though distributions are presented for clinical and normal populations, these are to be used as a guide in appreciating what high and low scores are like, but by no means can one say any given individual is neurotic or psychotic because his RIRS is low or high. The score has useful quantitative functions which we have tried to indicate. The score is useful to us clinically in helping to appreciate personality processes in our patients, but the score may not be interpreted mechanically.

NORMATIVE DATA: CHILDREN & ADOLESCENTS

Group Children:	Sex	Age	N	Median	Inter- quartile Range	Range
Gesell	Female	2	36	.74	.30–1.00	.00–2.23
	Male	2	30	.67	.30– .97	.00–1.53
	Female	3	33	1.05	.60–1.37	.10–2.18
	Male	3	31	1.00	.79–1.90	.20–4.08
	Female	4	37	1.25	.80–1.93	.30–4.70
	Male	4	38	1.19	.70–1.86	.27–5.33
	Female	5	44	1.22	.70–1.80	.30–3.23
	Male	5	44	1.60	1.20–1.83	.22–6.09
	Female	6	19	1.58	1.18–1.72	.70–5.00
Ledwith	Female	6	70	1.49	1.12–2.00	.40–3.75
Gesell	Male	6	21	1.44	1.14–2.27	.40–5.00
Ledwith	Male	6	69	1.35	.97–1.59	.50–2.58
Gesell	Female	7	20	1.73	1.30–1.92	1.00–4.27
Ledwith	Female	7	70	1.34	1.07–1.80	.50–5.75
Gesell	Male	7	22	2.00	1.00–2.54	.40–3.50
Ledwith	Male	7	69	1.43	1.07–1.56	.64–3.18
Gesell	Female	8	16	1.85	1.50–2.17	.90–3.20
Ledwith	Female	8	70	1.55	1.17–1.93	.40–3.25
Gesell	Male	8	22	2.00	1.35–2.73	.45–3.41
Ledwith	Male	8	69	1.43	1.13–1.92	.80–4.05
Gesell	Female	9	18	1.47	1.09–2.15	.41–3.18
Ledwith	Female	9	70	1.48	1.16–2.00	.50–5.25
Gesell	Male	9	21	2.08	1.33–3.19	.60–5.64
Ledwith	Male	9	69	1.55	1.23–1.91	.78–3.06
Gesell	Female	10	54	1.54	1.20–2.10	.30–5.40
Ledwith	Female	10	70	1.40	1.17–2.37	.50–5.75
Gesell	Male	10	43	1.75	1.20–2.20	.50–3.80
Ledwith	Male	10	69	1.48	1.10–1.98	.82–3.31
Gesell	Female	11	18	1.68	1.02–2.33	.64–3.33
Ledwith	Female	11	67	1.40	1.15–1.87	.50–5.25
Gesell	Male	11	34	1.92	1.50–2.45	1.00–4.09
Ledwith	Male	11	69	1.73	1.23–2.00	.76–4.41
Gesell	Female	12	22	1.83	1.29–2.60	.46–4.37
Gesell	Male	12	27	1.77	1.18–2.35	.94–3.09
Gesell	Female	13	22	1.59	.95–1.88	.38–2.78
Ledwith	Female	13	39	1.49	1.17–2.10	.89–5.37
Gesell	Male	13	18	1.59	1.10–2.00	.72–2.84
Ledwith	Male	13	38	1.50	1.13–2.08	.80–4.29
Gesell	Female	14	17	1.90	1.66–2.22	.50–3.00
Ledwith	Female	14	27	1.69	1.33–2.17	.90–3.82
Gesell	Male	14	23	1.60	1.14–2.00	.60–3.00
Ledwith	Male	14	22	1.65	1.32–2.08	1.14–3.76
Gesell	Female	15	25	1.42	1.18–2.08	.60–4.30
Gesell	Male	15	21	1.22	.90–1.66	.54–3.02
Gesell	Female	16	32	1.85	1.23–3.00	.81–6.80
Gesell	Male	16	27	1.27	1.00–1.70	.81–4.00
Quackenbush	Male	15-16	20	1.65	1.19–1.91	.33–3.12
Ledwith	Female	17	34	1.75	1.38–2.15	.87–6.35
Ledwith	Male	17	26	2.14	1.50–2.75	.94–4.24

NORMATIVE DATA: ADULTS—INDIVIDUAL RECORDS

Group	Sex	Age or Ed.	N	Median	Interquartile Range	Range
Army Personnel	Male	Young Adult	49	1.63	1.05–2.30	.72–4.50
Univ. No. Carolina	Male	College students	84	1.94	1.47–2.76	.87–7.35
Louisiana St. Univ.	26 Male 5 Female	Medical Students	31	2.23	1.86–3.13	1.27–4.10
N ach Ss (McClelland)	Male	College Students	30	2.56	1.79–3.77	1.28–6.50
Young Executives	Male	College Plus	20	3.28	2.70–4.05	1.62–5.29
Student Nurses	Female	Student Nurses	68	2.15	1.75–2.70	.95–4.25
"Levelers"	Female	College Students	10	2.07		1.02–3.71
"Sharpeners"	Female	College Students	10	2.61		2.03–4.31
Sensory Deprivation	Male	College Students	14	2.65		1.50–3.84

NORMATIVE DATA: ADULTS—GROUP RORSCHACHS

Group	Sex	Age or Ed.	N	Median	Interquartile Range	Range
Columbia Univ.	Female	20–52	49	2.10	1.68–2.83	.88–5.62
Columbia Univ.	Male	20–52	25	2.53	1.89–3.42	.83–3.68
Univ. Wisconsin	Female	Freshmen	34	3.38	2.57–4.42	1.68–7.57
Temple Univ.	Female	17–33	100	3.24	2.53–3.92	1.50–9.13
Penn State, Ogontz	Male	Psychol. Students	92	2.68	2.05–3.79	1.12–9.25
Penn State, Ogontz	Female	Psychol. Students	63	2.33	1.87–3.04	1.04–4.58
Ursinus	Male	Psychol. Students	74	2.88	2.10–4.17	1.45–10.73
Ursinus	Female	Psychol. Students	67	2.67	1.91–3.66	.96–6.41
Student Nurses	Female	Student Nurses	68	3.08	2.53–3.72	1.25–6.75
Male Nurses	Male	Young Adult	20	2.88	2.28–3.90	1.44–9.05

CLINICAL POPULATIONS—INDIVIDUAL RORSCHACHS

Group	Sex	Age or Ed.	N	Median	Inter-quartile Range	Range
Schizophrenics, Insulin treated	Male Female	15–44	18	1.25	1.00–2.06	.33–2.73
Schizophrenics, Negro	Female	Young Adult Median Ed. = HS	10	1.14	.54–1.97	.45–2.60
Schizophrenic, White	Female	Young Adult Median Ed. = HS plus	24	1.89	1.17–2.48	.77–4.87
Outpatient VA Neurotic	Male	Adult Superior Educ.	19	2.56	2.11–3.31	1.58–7.00
Outpatient VA Neurotic & Psychotic in Psychotherapy	Male	Adult Median Ed. = HS	50	1.93	1.37–2.60	.55–4.07
Adolescent Delinquent Upper income group	Male	13–19	23	1.97	1.40–2.47	1.10–3.12
Adolescent Delinquent Upper income Sex problems	Male	13–19	5	2.33		1.32–5.77
Adolescent Emot. Dist. Upper income	Female	14–19	41	2.00	1.49–2.68	.36–4.70
Adolescent Emot. Dist. Upper income	Male	13–19	54	2.00	1.49–2.78	.10–6.75
Text Book Hysterics	Female	Adult	8	1.87		1.26–2.90
Text Book Obsessive Compulsives	Male	Adult	8	3.46		2.04–5.15

VA Medical Patients

Group	Sex	Age or Ed.	N	Median	Inter-quartile Range	Range
Asthmatics	Male	23–67	20	1.31	.70–1.90	.20–3.15
Hypertensives	Male	28–67	19	1.36	.99–1.75	.40–2.83
Skin	Male	26–61	20	1.36	.73–1.80	.10–3.06
Ulcer	Male	27–69	21	1.50	1.10–2.00	.10–4.70
Mixed	Male	22–66	22	1.20	1.00–2.19	.63–3.00
Diabetics	Male	25–74	21	1.58	1.09–2.31	.60–4.45
Total Group	Male	22–74	123	1.33	1.00–1.91	.10–4.70

AUTHOR INDEX

SUBJECT INDEX